THE STORY OF
BASEBALL

>>

THE STORY OF
BASEBALL

>>

BY LAWRENCE S. RITTER
FOREWORD BY TED WILLIAMS

WILLIAM MORROW AND COMPANY
New York · 1983

NOTE TO THE READER: All records and current statistics in this book are as of the end of 1982. All historical statistics are from the fifth edition of *The Baseball Encyclopedia* (New York: Macmillan, 1982).

Printed in the United States of America.

1 2 3 4 5 6 7 8 9 10

Library of Congress Cataloging in Publication Data
Ritter, Lawrence S.   The story of baseball.
Summary: Traces the history of baseball, which was first played in a form resembling the modern game in Hoboken, New Jersey, in 1846, and first played by professional players in 1869. 1. Baseball—United States—History—Juvenile literature. [1. Baseball—History] I. Title.   GV863.A1R57   1983   796.357'0973   82-20367
ISBN 0-688-01724-X/ISBN 0-688-02066-6 (pbk.)

>>

For Elisabeth
with Love

> >>

FOREWORD

For a long time, I've been looking for a good book that explains the fundamentals of baseball to youngsters and introduces them to the great players of the past. Now I don't have to look any further, because Larry Ritter has come up with exactly what I've always wanted. *The Story of Baseball* is the perfect introduction to what baseball is all about.

You can't fully appreciate today's players unless you also know about the great stars who preceded them. When I was growing up in San Diego in the 1920s and early 1930s, Babe Ruth was the biggest name in baseball. Reading about him—and about others too, like Ty Cobb and Rogers Hornsby and Bill Terry—inspired me to try to be as good as they were. Looking back on it now, I don't think I ever felt as though I was just playing against nine men on an opposing team. I always had Ruth and Cobb and Hornsby and Terry way in the back of my mind. I think I was always trying to surpass them in the record books as much as I was trying to win that day's ballgame.

Tradition means a lot in baseball, which is one reason the game plays such a special role in American life. Babe Ruth, Lou Gehrig, and Jackie Robinson, for example, aren't only a part of baseball's past; they are an important part of America's history, too.

Just about all of Babe Ruth's records have been broken by now, but people still argue about whether Hank Aaron was a better home run hitter than the Babe. Just as they debate whether Walter Johnson was really the greatest pitcher of all time, and whether they would rather have Tris Speaker, Joe DiMaggio, or Willie Mays as their center fielder. Of course, there aren't any conclusive answers to such questions. But after you've finished *The Story of Baseball,* you'll at least have the background you need to form an intelligent opinion on these issues and on many others as well.

The chapters on hitting, pitching, fielding, and managing are the most interesting introductions to these subjects I've ever seen. This is a fun book. It is also informative, entertaining, and unique. Larry Ritter says he wrote it for youngsters, but whether you're 8 or 80, I think you'll love it. I know I did.

CONTENTS

PART ONE

Opening day, April 29, 1886, at the old Polo Grounds on Fifth Avenue and 110th Street in New York City. New York is playing Boston.

IN THE BEGINNING

Baseball has been providing us with fun and excitement for more than a hundred years. The first game resembling baseball as we know it today was played in Hoboken, New Jersey, on June 19, 1846. The New York Nine beat the New York Knickerbockers that day, 23-1.

The game was played according to rules drawn up by Alexander J. Cartwright, a surveyor and amateur athlete. Although many people believe otherwise, it is a myth that Abner Doubleday invented baseball. It was Alexander Cartwright, not Abner Doubleday, who first laid out the present dimensions of the playing field and established the basic rules of the game.

The first *professional* baseball team was the Cincinnati Red Stockings, who toured the country in 1869 and didn't lose a game all year. Soon, baseball began to attract so many fans that in 1876 the National League was organized—the same National League that still exists today.

Although the game as it was played in 1876 was recognizable as baseball—nobody would confuse it with football or basketball—it was quite a bit different from baseball as we know it now. For example, pitchers had to throw underhand, the way they still do in softball; the batter could request the pitcher to throw a "high" or "low" pitch; it took 9 balls, rather than 4, for a batter to get a base on balls; and the pitching distance was only 45 feet to home plate.

The rules were gradually changed over the following twenty years, until by about 1900 the game was more or less the same as it is today. In 1884, pitchers were permitted to throw overhand; in 1887, the batter was no longer allowed to request a "high" or "low" pitch; by 1889, it took only 4 balls for a batter to get a base on balls; and, in 1893, the pitching distance was lengthened to the present 60 feet, 6 inches.

Players didn't start to wear gloves on the field until the 1880s. At first, they wore only a thin piece of leather over the palm of the hand, with five holes cut out for the fingers to go through. By the 1890s, however, the gloves began to look like today's baseball gloves, although they were not nearly as large.

Gloves remained more or less the same from around 1900 to the mid-1950s. The ball was caught in the "pocket" of the glove, covering the palm of the hand, and it was held with the fingers. The fingers of the glove were short and fairly flexible. The only purpose of the glove was to protect the palm and fingers from injury, although until the 1930s many players insisted on cutting a rather large hole in the palm of the glove in order to grip the ball better.

Nowadays, the glove is much larger than it used to be, and the ball is not caught in the palm of the hand but trapped in the glove's webbing, between the thumb and forefinger. Since the mid-1950s, the glove has become more of a net with which to snare the ball rather than just a protective covering for the hand.

The baseball fields were nowhere near as well taken care of as they are now, so that it was not at all unusual in the old days for the ball to take bad bounces because of pebbles in the infield or uneven ground in the outfield.

Sometimes the ball took a crazy bounce because it was a little lopsided. Since only two or three baseballs would be used for a whole game, by the seventh or eighth inning the ball was often in pretty bad shape. Indeed, this was true until the 1920s. If a ball, like a foul ball or a home run, went into the stands, the ushers would try to get it back, sometimes offering whoever had it a free pass to another game. If the ushers succeeded in getting it back, it would be returned to the field, and the game would resume with the same ball. Now, of course, fifty or sixty baseballs are used in an average big league game.

Until the early 1900s, one umpire took care of the entire field. Typically, he would call balls and strikes from behind the catcher until a man got on base, and then move out and call balls and strikes from behind the pitcher so he could be closer to the bases in case of an attempted steal.

With only one umpire, there was plenty of opportunity for mischief. A favorite trick was pulled by a man who was on second base, with the umpire working from behind the pitcher. If the batter got a hit to right field, the umpire would have to watch the ball and possibly the batter rounding first base and trying for second. Meanwhile, the man who had been on base would veer off toward home before he got as far as third, never coming anywhere close to the base.

Tim Hurst, a famous umpire in the 1890s who knew all the tricks of the trade, once called a player out who slid across home plate in a cloud of dust even though no one was even trying to tag him. Tim had been looking toward right field and second base all the while, but then he whirled around and yelled, "You're out!"

"What do you mean I'm out?" the player screamed. "They didn't even make a play on me."

"You never touched third base," Tim shouted back.

"Of course, I did," the player responded. "And anyway, how do *you* know? You weren't even watching."

"That's just it," the umpire said. "For when I wasn't watching, you got home *too* fast!"

Needless to say, Tim Hurst won the argument, as have all umpires before and since.

In 1901, a second major league, the American League, was established alongside the twenty-five-year-old National League. Many of the stars of the National League jumped over to the new American League because they were offered higher salaries. Ballplayers didn't make the kind of money in those days that they make now, of course, but even then financial matters were an important part of professional baseball.

After some initial hard feelings, the pennant winners of the two major leagues met each other in 1903 in the first modern World Series. The stage was set for a great and long-lasting rivalry, one that continues to this very day.

1900-1920

Matty, Honus, Ty, and Walter

Modern baseball dates from about 1900. The four greatest players in the early years—from 1900 to 1920—were Christy Mathewson, Honus Wagner, Ty Cobb, and Walter Johnson. Mathewson and Walter Johnson were pitchers, Honus Wagner was a shortstop, and Ty Cobb was an outfielder.

Everyone agrees that in general athletes are better today than they were many years ago. They are bigger, stronger, and faster. Even so, everyone who saw them also agrees that if Matty, Honus, Ty, and Walter could somehow magically return today, they would be as great now as they were then.

Although the rules of the game haven't changed much since 1900, something else has: at that time, ballplayers were looked down upon by the general public. They were considered uneducated roughnecks, not good enough to associate with respectable people. They were treated like second-class citizens.

Many years later, Sam Crawford, a great outfielder with the Detroit Tigers in the early 1900s, told a friend what it used to be like then. "Baseball players weren't too much accepted in those days," he said. "In fact, we were considered to be pretty crude. When we traveled to play in other cities, for example, they wouldn't let us in the best hotels most of the time. And when we did manage to get into a good hotel, they wouldn't boast about having us. Like if we went into the hotel dining room, they'd shove us way in the back so we wouldn't be too conspicuous."

Sam thought for a moment and then laughed. "I remember when I was with the Detroit team in 1903, one evening we all went into the dining room of this fancy hotel in St. Louis. The dining room had a tile floor made out of little square tiles. We sat there—way in the back, as usual—for about twenty minutes and couldn't get any waiters. They wouldn't pay any attention to us. Well, finally, our shortstop said he knew how we could get a waiter. And I'll be darned if he didn't take one of the plates off the table and toss it way up in the air. When it came down on that tile floor, it smashed into a million pieces. Sure enough, we had four or five waiters around there in no time."

The public's opinion of ballplayers as rowdies, roughnecks, and punks disappeared between 1905 and 1910 due in large part to the efforts of three men.

They were John J. McGraw, the fiery manager of the New York Giants; Connie Mack (his real name was Cornelius McGilli-cuddy), the kindly manager of the Philadelphia Athletics; and Christy Mathewson, the greatest pitcher of his day.

Managers John McGraw and Connie Mack insisted that their players act like gentlemen and dress in suits and ties when they were off the field. Once they had accomplished this, they repeat-edly asked the best hotels and restaurants to accept their teams. Eventually, they succeeded in gaining admittance just about everywhere.

Christy Mathewson helped change the public's attitude toward ballplayers by the example he set, always conducting himself with dignity and respect for others both on and off the field. He was so idolized throughout the country that people started thinking that if he was a baseball player, then baseball players must be okay.

Christy
Mathewson
in 1901

Matty warming up

Christy Mathewson was born in 1880 in Factoryville, Pennsylvania. He went to Bucknell University, where he played football as well as baseball. He was also an honor student and a member of the glee club and the college literary society. Handsome, modest, a superb athlete, he was the original all-American boy, and by his behavior and his pitching he became the idol of millions.

Matty's pitching feats are legendary. Thirteen times he won 20 or more games, and in four of those seasons he won 30 or more. In 1905, he won 31 games and lost only 8, and in 1908 he won 37 and lost only 11. He was untouchable in the 1905 World Series, winning 3 games in the space of six days and not allowing a single run in any of them. Over his career, which stretched from 1900 to 1916, almost all with the New York Giants, he won a total of 373 games.

He achieved his success against opposing batters with a fast ball, a sharp-breaking curve, and a reverse curve that he called his "fadeaway." Mathewson was a right-handed pitcher, and an ordinary curve thrown by a right-handed pitcher curves *away from* a right-handed batter. But Matty's reverse curve, or fadeaway, curved *in toward* a right-handed batter, not away from him. Today such a pitch would be called a screwball.

For many years, Mathewson's catcher was Chief John Tortes Meyers, a Cahuilla Indian from Southern California, who was the Giants' regular catcher from 1909 to 1915. Years later, when he was over eighty years old, Chief Meyers recalled what Matty was like in those days:

"How we loved to play for that guy! We'd break our necks for him. If you made an error behind him, or anything of that sort, he'd never get mad or sulk. He'd come over and pat you on the back. He had the sweetest, most gentle nature. Did you know that he was a great checkers player, too? He was checkers champion of half a dozen states. He'd play checkers with ten or twelve opponents all at once and beat every one of them. Actually, that's what made him such a great pitcher—his wonderful retentive memory combined with his great control. Anytime someone hit a ball hard off of him, you can bet that fellow never got another pitch in the same spot again.''

One of Mathewson's toughest opponents—not in checkers but in the batter's box—was Honus Wagner, the hard-hitting shortstop for the Pittsburgh Pirates. There has never been a shortstop, before or since, who could hit like Wagner.

Most shortstops are noted more for their fielding than for their hitting. But Wagner's batting average was .300 or better for *seventeen* consecutive seasons, and he led the National League in batting a record eight times. (If you are not an expert on batting averages, the first few pages of chapter 6 discuss what they mean and how to calculate them.)

If Honus Wagner didn't hit like a typical shortstop, he didn't look like one, either. Most shortstops are slim and graceful. Not Honus. He was built more like a weight lifter. A bit under 6 feet tall, he weighed a solid 200 pounds and was as bowlegged as a cowboy who has spent all his life on horseback. Nevertheless, he was remarkably fast for a big man, as shown by the 722 bases he stole in his career.

Honus didn't glide around the infield like a greyhound, making hard plays look easy. Quite the opposite. He looked more like a grizzly bear, scrambling after any ball hit in his direction, scooping it up with his huge hands, along with any dirt that happened to get in the way, and firing the whole thing over to first base— dirt and all. It didn't look too smooth or graceful, but it must have been effective because most experts consider him the greatest all-around shortstop who ever lived.

Wagner was a more sociable person than Mathewson. While

Honus Wagner
in 1908

Matty was reserved and shy, especially with people he didn't know, Honus was friendly and talkative. He was always ready to stop and chat, even with strangers. This made him extremely popular with the fans not only in Pittsburgh—where he was born and played most of his career—but in every other city around the league as well.

One thing Honus did *not* like, however, was cigarettes. In those days, baseball cards often came with packs of cigarettes, the same way they now come with bubble gum. In 1909, without his knowledge, a cigarette company issued a Honus Wagner card with his picture on the front and the name of the cigarette on the back. Honus refused to be associated with cigarettes in any way. As soon as he found out about it, he demanded that all the cards still in the stores be withdrawn and destroyed.

As a result, only a few are known to exist today. Because they are so rare, collectors of old baseball cards now value them at many thousands of dollars each. To be precise, in 1982, a 1909 Honus Wagner card in perfect condition was worth $25,000!

After his great playing career ended in 1917, Honus became a coach with the Pirates, a position he held until he retired in 1951 at the age of seventy-seven. As he grew older, he enjoyed telling stories about his playing days, many of which are hard to believe, to say the least.

One of his favorites was about when he was called on to pinch-hit one day with the score tied in the bottom half of the ninth inning. "I hit a home run," Honus would say, "but I was so excited that I ran around the bases the wrong way, starting at third base, and when I crossed home plate, they subtracted a run, and we lost the game!"

Another was about the time he was reaching for a ground ball and instead of the ball grabbed a rabbit that had just run onto the field. "I threw the rabbit to first base," said Honus, "and got the runner by a hare!"

Although Wagner hit .300 or better for seventeen consecutive years and led the National League in batting eight times, he was not the greatest hitter of his time. That honor goes to Tyrus Raymond Cobb, who was the greatest hitter of *all* time.

Ty Cobb hit over .300 for an amazing *twenty-three* consecutive years, spanning the period from 1906 through 1928. In three of those years, he did something only seven others have accomplished since 1900—he hit over .400. His batting average was .420 in 1911, .410 in 1912, and .401 in 1922.

He led the American League in batting a record *twelve* times, and his *lifetime* batting average, over his long career, was a phenomenal .367. No one else has ever come close to that figure. (Honus Wagner's lifetime batting average was .329.) Cobb also holds the record for the most lifetime base hits—4,191. In the entire history of baseball, no hitter has ever been in his class.

Ty Cobb was born in a small town in Georgia in 1886. He threw right-handed but batted left-handed. He held his hands a few inches apart on the bat and learned to bunt or slap line-drive hits precisely where he wanted them. He made place hitting an art.

After a couple of seasons in the minor leagues, he joined the Detroit Tigers as an outfielder in August 1905, four months short of his nineteenth birthday. Two years later, he hit .350 and led the American League in batting average, hits, runs batted in, and stolen bases.

From then on, the "Georgia Peach" only improved with time. In 1927, at the age of forty, he was still able to hit .357 and steal 22 bases.

Forty years later, in 1967, a youngster asked Lefty O'Doul, who also had been a great hitter, what he thought Ty Cobb would hit now, playing under present-day conditions.

"Oh, I'd say he'd hit about .320 or so," O'Doul replied.

"Then why do you say Cobb was so great?" the youngster

Ty Cobb

asked. "After all, there are half a dozen players around who can hit .320."

"Well," O'Doul answered, "you have to take into consideration the man would now be eighty years old!"

Cobb was particularly dangerous in the late innings of a close game because he was always a threat to break it open single-handedly. Not with a home run, because that wasn't his style. Instead, he did it with speed, cleverness, deception, and intimidation.

His specialty was a perfectly placed bunt to get on first base . . . soon he would be taking a long lead off the base to distract the pitcher . . . a sudden dash for second, spikes flying, and a fallaway slide to avoid the second baseman's tag . . . sprinting to third base on a wild pickoff attempt by a nervous pitcher . . . and then, amid mounting tension, the final climax . . . a false start . . . another false start . . . and a blur on the basepath, a cloud of dust, and a spikes-high slide over home plate.

Ty Cobb successfully stole home a record *thirty-five* times!

He stole 96 bases in 1915, which remained the single-season record for stolen bases until 1962. Over his entire career, he stole 892 bases, which was the lifetime record for stolen bases for fifty years, until it was finally surpassed by Lou Brock in 1977.

Ty Cobb was the greatest and most exciting player of his generation, perhaps of all time. Unfortunately, he was also the most *disliked* player of his generation, perhaps of all time.

From all reports, he was mean, selfish, arrogant, and bigoted. His fierce determination to be number one, to win no matter what it cost, left little room for kindness, compassion, or friendship.

Ty Cobb sliding into third. The year is 1909 and the third baseman is Jimmy Austin.

Davy Jones played in the Detroit outfield next to Cobb for seven years, from 1906 through 1912. Many years later, he talked about Ty's personality.

"The trouble was," he said, "Cobb had such a rotten disposition it was hard to be his friend. He antagonized so many people hardly anyone would speak to him, even among his own teammates. Ty didn't have a sense of humor. Especially, he could never laugh at himself. Consequently, he took a lot of things the wrong way. What usually would be an innocent wisecrack would start a fistfight if Ty was involved. It was too bad. He was one of the greatest players who ever lived, and yet he had so few friends. I always felt sorry for him."

In his older years, Cobb mellowed somewhat. But it was too late. When he died, in 1961, only three men from all of major league baseball attended his funeral.

In terms of personality, the modest Walter Johnson was another story altogether. Born in Kansas in 1887, he joined the Washington Senators in the American League in 1907. He remained there for twenty years, never pitching for anyone else. He hit his stride in 1910 when he won 25 games for a next-to-last-place team. He won 20 or more games a dozen times, including more than 30 in both 1912 and 1913.

Walter rarely pitched with a decent team behind him. In those days, a popular joke was that Washington was first in war, first in peace, and last in the American League. Even with such poor support, Walter Johnson is the *all-time leader in games won in the twentieth century,* with 416 victories—43 more than Christy Mathewson. (The legendary Cy Young won over 500 games, but he won most of them before 1900.)

Walter is also the all-time leader in shutouts, with 113. Actually, the Washington team scored so few runs that he often *had* to pitch a shutout to win.

He won most of those 416 games with just one kind of pitch—a jet-propelled fast ball. Late in his career, he developed a curve, but it was never very good. It didn't matter, though, because his fast ball was enough. The batters knew what was coming, but they still couldn't hit it. Often, they said, they couldn't even see it.

One of baseball's classic stories takes place on an overcast September afternoon when Walter Johnson and his catcher decided to try an experiment. It was said so often that Walter's pitches were too fast to see that they decided to find out what would happen if a pitch *really* couldn't be seen.

Conditions were perfect for the experiment. It was late in the afternoon, with darkness starting to fall, so that it was hard to see the ball, anyway. And it was the bottom half of the ninth inning, with two outs and two strikes on the batter. One more strike and the game would be over.

The catcher walked out to the pitcher's mound for a conference with Johnson, and when he returned to his position behind home plate, he had the ball with him—concealed in his big catcher's mitt.

Walter Johnson stepped on the mound, wound up, and went through his complete pitching motion. An instant after he apparently threw the ball, the catcher smacked it loudly into the center of his mitt and then moved his bare hand away so that the ball was plainly visible.

"Strike three!" the umpire shouted with just a moment's hesitation. Mumbling to himself, the batter turned toward his dugout, and so ended the ball game.

Was Walter Johnson the fastest pitcher who ever lived? Old-timers swear he was and speak of his speed with awe. Others say that Lefty Grove or Bob Feller or Sandy Koufax or Nolan Ryan was even faster.

There is no way to really settle the argument, but what *is* certain is that Walter Johnson struck out a total of 3,508 opponents, twelve times leading the league in strikeouts. It is more than fifty

Walter
Johnson
in 1908

years since he retired, and those achievements are still unsurpassed (although Nolan Ryan will probably exceed 3,508 strikeouts soon).

Humble, generous, good-natured, Walter always worried that he might injure a batter with his fast ball. Regardless of the provocation, he would never deliberately throw at anyone. Like Honus Wagner, he was popular with players and fans throughout the league. Indeed, near the end of his career, most fans seemed to think it was a privilege just to see him pitch regardless of whether their team won or lost.

Walter Johnson, left, and teammate Clyde Milan. The year is 1913, when Walter won 36 games and lost only 7, and Milan hit .301 and stole 75 bases.

In 1936, nine years after he had stopped pitching, Walter Johnson came out of retirement to make one more historic throw. He agreed to try to duplicate George Washington's celebrated feat of throwing a silver dollar across the Rappahannock River at Fredericksburg, Virginia. Standing on the river bank, his shoes in the mud, Johnson wound up and was short with his first attempt. He wound up again, and this time made it with plenty to spare.

The length of his throw was estimated at 317 feet. With characteristic modesty, he said, "I guess the river must be narrower than in George Washington's time."

By the early 1900s, the rules of the game had evolved into just about what they are now. However, although the rules were about the same as now, the way the game was actually played was something else again.

The game was played differently then simply because the ball was different. It *looked* just like today's baseball, but when it was hit, no matter how hard, it did not carry long distances. Balls were hardly ever hit over the fence for a home run.

In 1908, Detroit's Sam Crawford led the American League in home runs with only 7. In 1909, Ty Cobb led with 9. And most of those didn't go over the fence. They were inside-the-park homers, where the ball got past the outfielders, and the batter made it around the bases before they could throw it back in.

With such a dead ball, batters didn't swing with all their might trying to hit home runs. Instead, they practiced bunting and place hitting. They became expert at punching line drives over the shortstop's head and slapping hard ground balls between the first and second basemen.

Wee Willie Keeler, who was 5 feet 4½ inches tall and weighed 140 pounds soaking wet, put it in a nutshell when he said, "I try to hit 'em where they ain't."

Under the circumstances, strategy was more important than power in baseball's early years. Teams tried to get one run at a time by bunting, place hitting, base stealing, and outthinking the opposition. Brains were as important as brawn, maybe more so.

This type of game captured the imagination of the country and grew tremendously popular. The same ballplayers who couldn't get into a decent hotel in 1900 were hailed as celebrities a decade later. By the time the United States entered World War I, in 1917, baseball had become recognized throughout the land as America's national pastime. No other sport or form of entertainment was even close.

And then, in 1920, the game changed dramatically. It suddenly switched from strategy to power, from brains to brawn. The change was due to one man and one man only. His name was Babe Ruth.

1920-1940

Babe Ruth and the Lively Ball

Babe Ruth changed the game of baseball dramatically and permanently. Even with the dead ball, the young Babe Ruth hit skyscraper-high home runs that amazed his teammates and opponents as much as the fans. No one had ever hit the ball so high and so far before. Fans packed the ballparks to see him hit one over the fence.

Impressed by his popularity, the team owners decided to cash in on it. If the fans wanted to see home runs, then that's what they'd get. So, without any publicity, in 1920, the owners quietly got rid of the dead ball and substituted a new lively one in its place. It looked just like the dead ball, but when it was hit, it traveled a lot farther.

Baseball has never been the same since.

Within a decade, home runs started to become routine. Formerly as rare as diamonds, they became commonplace. At the same time, the arts of bunting and place hitting went into a fifty-year decline. The strategy and tactics of playing for one run at a time gave way to swinging for the fences, as teams tried to get runs quickly and in bunches.

Today, Babe Ruth is remembered primarily as a home-run hit-

25

Babe Ruth

ter. That he was, indeed, but he was much more as well. For example, over his twenty-two-year career, he compiled a .342 lifetime batting average, *seventh highest* in twentieth-century baseball history. While it is true that Hank Aaron eventually did hit 41 more lifetime home runs than Babe Ruth—755 for Aaron to 714 for Ruth—Aaron needed approximately *four thousand* more times at bat to do it.

The main reason Ruth came to bat so many times fewer than Aaron was because for the first five years Ruth was in the big leagues—from 1914 through 1918 with the Boston Red Sox—he was a *pitcher,* playing only every fourth or fifth day.

He was, in fact, the *best* left-handed pitcher in baseball at the time. As a pitcher, he won 23 games in 1916 and 24 in 1917. In 1918, when the Red Sox began to put him in the outfield so he could play more often, he won 13 games as a pitcher and simultaneously tied for the major league lead in home runs!

George Herman Ruth was born in 1895 in the slums of Baltimore, Maryland. At the age of seven, because of chronic truancy and disciplinary problems, he was sent to a Baltimore home for hard-to-control boys, St. Mary's Industrial School for Boys. It was run by the Catholic Xaverian Brothers.

He was in and out of St. Mary's for twelve years, until, at the age of nineteen, he finally left for good to play professional baseball. In later years, he always said that St. Mary's had been his real home and spoke of it with great fondness.

He came to the Boston Red Sox in 1914 as a left-handed pitcher. It was as a left-handed hitter, though, that he began to attract special attention. He hit so well that by 1919 the Red Sox decided to take their best pitcher and convert him into a full-time outfielder in order to get his bat in the line-up every day.

Harry Hooper was a star Boston outfielder when Babe Ruth first joined the Red Sox. Many years later, he talked about what Ruth was like back then.

"You probably remember him," Hooper said, "with that big belly he got later on. But that wasn't there in the early days. George was 6 feet 2 inches tall and weighed 198 pounds, all of it muscle. He had a slim waist, huge biceps, no self-discipline, and not much education—not very different from lots of other young ballplayers in those days. Except for two things: he could hit a baseball further than anyone else, and he could eat more.

"Lord," Hooper recalled, "he certainly did eat too much. He'd order half a dozen hot dogs, as many bottles of soda pop, and stuff them in one after the other. That would hold him for a couple of hours, and then he'd be at it again."

In January 1920, the Boston Red Sox sold Babe Ruth to the New York Yankees for $125,000, surely the most foolish deal ever made in the history of baseball. In 1919, as a full-time outfielder, Ruth had set a new single-season home run record with 29 homers. In 1920, with the Yankees and the new lively ball, he zoomed to 54 home runs; and in 1921, to 59. These would be considered remarkable home-run totals even now. In those days, they were unbelievable!

With the introduction of the new lively ball, others started to clout home runs over the fence, too. But not like the Babe. In 1920, when he led the American League with 54 home runs, the runner-up had only 19. No other *team* in the league, aside from the Yankees, had as many home runs as Babe Ruth had all by himself. In 1921, when he led the league with 59, the runner-up had only 24.

In addition, in 1920, Ruth batted .376 and drove in 137 runs. In 1921, he hit .378 and drove in 171 runs. He proceeded to lead the league in home runs a dozen times, in runs scored eight times, and in runs batted in six times.

In the 1920s, Babe Ruth was idolized by millions, the greatest sports figure in America. He was Superman. When he hit 60 home runs in 1927 to set his famous record, it didn't create any special excitement. After all, everybody thought, he's only breaking his own record; next year, he'll probably break it again.

It did cause some controversy, however, when his salary reached $80,000 in 1930 and exceeded that of President Herbert Hoover. That was a huge sum in those days, when ballplayers didn't make anything like the kind of money they make today. When asked how he could possibly justify making more money than the president of the United States, Ruth replied in words that have been quoted ever since. "I had a better year than he did," said the Babe.

But no one can go on forever, and by 1935 Babe Ruth had reached the end of the trail. He was forty years old, more overweight than usual, could no longer run well, and his batting eye was fading. The Yankees released him in February and urged him to retire. He refused and tried to hang on with Boston in the National League, back in the city where his career had started twenty-one years earlier. But he had little success, and in May 1935, with a batting average less than his weight, he reluctantly accepted the inevitable and called it quits.

Five days before he retired, though, he turned the clock back—it had to be by sheer will power—and gave one last glorious display of Ruthian fireworks. On May 25, at Pittsburgh's Forbes Field he hit three mighty home runs in one game. The third, measured at over 600 feet on the fly, is the longest ever hit in that ballpark.

Appropriately, it turned out to be his final big league hit. He trotted around the bases for what would be the last time to a thunderous ovation—although as many fans seemed to be crying as cheering.

No matter how great his fame, Babe Ruth never forgot his youth at St. Mary's Industrial School for Boys. Regardless of the demands on his time, he spent countless hours cheering up youngsters in hospitals and orphanages in New York and wherever the Yankees traveled. It was often said that he appeared to be

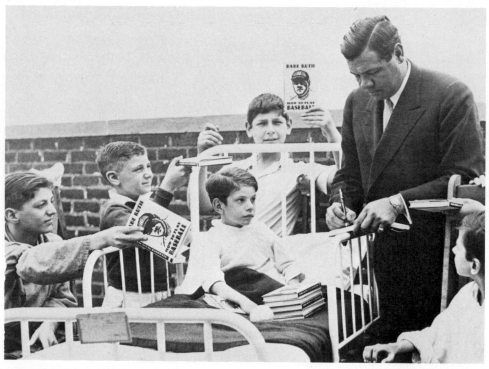

Babe Ruth and friends

more at ease with children than with adults—perhaps because he was just a big kid himself—and youngsters everywhere spontaneously returned his affection.

Only thirteen years after he stopped playing, George Herman Ruth died of cancer at the relatively young age of fifty-three. The sorrow that was felt throughout the country was deep and genuine. Looking back even today, teammates and opponents almost universally say that knowing him was one of the high points of their lives.

Jimmy Austin, a long-time third baseman in the American League, played against Ruth many times. The depth of his feelings, expressed in an interview many years later, is typical of those who played with or against the Babe.

"What a warmhearted, generous soul he was," Austin said. "He was always friendly, always had time for a laugh or a wisecrack. The Babe always had a twinkle in his eye, and when he hit a homer against us, he'd never trot past third without giving me a wink. The big guy wasn't perfect. Everybody knows that. But he had a heart, he really did. A heart as big as a watermelon and made out of pure gold."

Powered by Ruth's booming bat, the New York Yankees began the dynasty that brought them eleven American League pennants and eight World Championships during the 1920s and 1930s. Ruth dominated the game and everyone in it, including many outstanding players who would have attained much greater fame were they not playing under his long shadow: for example, men such as Grover Cleveland Alexander, Rogers Hornsby, and Lou Gehrig, to name only three.

Grover Cleveland Alexander ranks with Walter Johnson and

Grover Cleveland Alexander

Christy Mathewson among the greatest pitchers of all time. A lanky, freckle-faced farm boy from Nebraska, he won 373 games during his twenty-year career with the Philadelphia Phillies, Chicago Cubs, and St. Louis Cardinals. That ties him with Mathewson for second place in lifetime wins in the twentieth century, topped only by Walter Johnson's 416.

A right-handed pitcher with a sneaky fast ball, a deceptive curve, and amazing control, Alexander won 30 or more games three years in a row, from 1915 through 1917. In six other years, he won more than 20 games. In 1916, 16 of his victories were shutouts, which is still a record.

Alexander's courage was extraordinary. He had epilepsy and achieved his remarkable record despite the ever-present threat of an epileptic seizure. At that time, there was no medication available to prevent such attacks.

Hans Lobert was the Philadelphia Phillies' third baseman for a number of years when Alex was their star pitcher. "His big problem," recalled Lobert, "was that he had epileptic fits maybe two or three times a season. He'd froth at the mouth and shiver all over and thrash around and lose consciousness. We'd hold him down and open his mouth and grab his tongue to keep him from choking himself. After a while, he'd be all right. During the years I was there, it only happened on the bench, never out on the pitching mound."

Alexander also suffered from alcoholism, which eventually destroyed him. He died in 1950 at the age of sixty-three. Two years later, Hollywood made *The Winning Team,* a movie about his life. The role of Grover Cleveland Alexander, who had been named after our twenty-second president, was played by our fortieth, Ronald Reagan.

Rogers Hornsby ranks right below Ty Cobb as baseball's all-time greatest hitter. His *lifetime* batting average of .358, over a twenty-three-year career, is second only to Cobb's .367. Since Hornsby batted right-handed and Cobb left-handed, he has the honor of being the best right-handed hitter in the game's history.

Rogers Hornsby was born in 1896 in Winters, Texas, and he had the cold gray eyes of an old-time Texas gunfighter. Those eyes became something of an obsession. He refused to read books or go to the movies for fear it would harm his eyes and affect his hitting.

Rogers Hornsby in 1920, when he hit "only" .370

Hornsby, a second baseman, led the National League in batting seven times, including a phenomenal five-year period from 1921 through 1925 when he hit (believe it or not) .397, .401, .384, .424, and .403. For the five years taken together, this averages out at .402. Even Ty Cobb never had five consecutive years quite *that* good! Aside from Hornsby and Cobb, no one else has ever hit over .400 *three* times.

But it was Rogers Hornsby's misfortune to have his career coincide with Babe Ruth's. Since Hornsby was not primarily a home-run slugger—although he did lead the league in homers twice—all the publicity went to Ruth. Also, Hornsby was not a very colorful player, whereas the Babe was larger than life in everything he did.

Hornsby came to the major leagues in 1915 with the St. Louis Cardinals, with whom he played until 1926. Thereafter, he was traded frequently, despite his spectacular batting averages, because he was a grouchy and tactless sort of fellow who had trouble getting along with people—especially managers and owners. Later, he became a manager himself as well as a part owner, and then he had similar trouble getting along with his own players.

But it is obvious from his .358 lifetime batting average that he never had much trouble getting along with opposing pitchers. Asked once if he ever feared any pitcher, he answered, "No, I feel sorry for them." Those who knew him said he wasn't boasting. In his typical blunt fashion, he was just being honest.

Lou Gehrig was the classic case of playing in Babe Ruth's shadow. As the New York Yankees' first baseman from 1925 through 1938, there was no way he could escape the big man be-

Lou Gehrig

hind him in right field. However, this never seemed to bother Gehrig. He was a shy, modest person who was content to leave the spotlight to Ruth.

Gehrig was born in New York City in 1903. After attending Columbia University, where he waited on tables to pay his way through school, he joined the Yankees in 1925 and soon became one of baseball's outstanding hitters. He is remembered by the public mainly as the durable Iron Horse who played in 2,130 consecutive games between 1925 and 1939. His teammates and opponents, however, remember him more for his blistering line drives and his ability to drive in runs.

For thirteen consecutive seasons, he batted in over 100 runs, seven of those times over 150, including 1931, when he drove in 184 runs, an American League record. He batted in a lifetime total of 1,990 runs, more than anyone in baseball history except Hank Aaron (who had 2,297) and Babe Ruth (who had 2,204). Had illness not cut him down prematurely, he probably would have added another 308, enough to top them both.

One indication of his effectiveness when he came to bat with men on base is the 23 home runs he hit *with the bases loaded,* an all-time major league record.

He hit over 40 home runs five times and batted over .340 eight times. A left-handed hitter, his lifetime batting average was a notable .340, tenth highest in the twentieth century.

Gehrig usually batted fourth in the Yankee batting order, right behind Babe Ruth. A reporter once mentioned to him that no matter what Gehrig did, he seemed to get almost no publicity.

Lou laughed and said, "I'm not a headline guy, and we might as well face it. When the Babe's turn at bat is over, whether he belted a homer or struck out, the fans are still talking about it when I come up. Heck, nobody would notice if I stood on my head at home plate.''

On May 1, 1939, after playing in an unbelievable 2,130 consecutive games stretching over fourteen years, Lou Gehrig took himself out of the Yankee line-up for the good of the team. He felt weak and uncoordinated. Doctors discovered that he was suffering from an incurable rare illness, amyotrophic lateral sclerosis, now called Lou Gehrig's disease, which destroys the central nervous system. The gentle first baseman died two years later, a couple of weeks before his thirty-eighth birthday.

A widely praised 1942 movie about Lou Gehrig's life, starring Gary Cooper, was named *The Pride of the Yankees*. The dictionary defines ''pride'' in this sense as ''someone to be proud of . . . the best in a group.'' The movie could not have been better named.

During the 1930s, a number of power hitters took dead aim at Babe Ruth's record of 60 home runs in a season, which he had set in 1927, and tried their best to topple it.

Chicago Cubs' outfielder Hack Wilson was the first to come close. Hack had an unlikely build for a baseball player—he was 5 feet 6 inches tall and weighed 195 pounds—but he could hit a baseball prodigious distances. He played with eagerness and enthusiasm and was a tremendous favorite with the fans.

In 1930, Hack hit 56 home runs, still the most anyone has ever hit in the National League. He fell four short of Ruth's 60, but he did set an all-time record for runs batted in that year, with the astounding total of 190.

Two great first basemen were the next to try. In 1932, Jimmie

Hack Wilson was only five feet six inches tall, but he weighed close to 200 pounds, and when he swung the earth trembled. This is 1930, the year he hit 56 home runs and drove in 190 runs.

Foxx of the Philadelphia Athletics reached 58, and Hank Greenberg of the Detroit Tigers matched that figure in 1938.

Aside from Roger Maris, who finally surpassed the Babe in 1961, no one else has ever hit as many as 55 home runs in one season. Indeed, only five others have ever reached the 50 mark—

(right)
Jimmie Foxx: over 20
years, 534 career
home runs and a .325
lifetime batting aver-
age

(below)
Two great first base-
men: Lou Gehrig, left,
and Hank Greenberg

Ralph Kiner, Willie Mays, Mickey Mantle, Johnny Mize, and George Foster. (Kiner, Mays, and Mantle did it twice.)

As the 1930s came to an end, there were two revolutionary innovations that would ultimately affect almost every aspect of the game: night baseball and television.

The first big league night game was played on May 24, 1935, when President Franklin Delano Roosevelt pushed a button in the White House that turned on the lights in Cincinnati for a night game between the Cincinnati Reds and the Philadelphia Phillies.

Most of the owners were not very enthusiastic about the idea at first. "There is no chance of night baseball ever becoming popular," one of them said, "because high-class baseball cannot be played under artificial light." But when they saw how attendance increased when games were scheduled at night, they changed their minds.

The first night game in Brooklyn turned out to be more spectacular than expected because Cincinnati pitcher Johnny Vander Meer pitched a no-hitter against the Dodgers. In his previous appearance, four days earlier, Vander Meer had also pitched a no-hitter. He remains the only pitcher in baseball history to throw two no-hitters in succession.

August 26, 1939, was the occasion for the first television coverage of a major league ballgame. An experimental telecast was made that day of a Cincinnati-Brooklyn game played in Brooklyn. It was reported that the game could be seen on a television set "as far away as fifty miles." Hardly anyone took it seriously because television was then considered little more than a toy.

Once television really became widespread, in the 1950s and

1960s, it had a dramatic impact on baseball, especially on players' salaries and the minor leagues. Salaries began to skyrocket because the players moved into the category of TV stars. On the other hand, the minor leagues were decimated because fans chose to watch big league games on TV instead of going out to minor league ballparks. In 1949, there were 59 minor leagues, with 464 teams. By 1980, only 17 minor leagues remained, with but 155 teams. Almost all the current minor league teams are "farm clubs" of a big league team and are heavily subsidized by their major league parent.

Sad to say, at the end of the 1930s, one thing remained unchanged: by unwritten agreement of the team owners, black ballplayers were still not permitted to play in the major or minor leagues. This discrimination had nothing to do with ability. Black ballplayers were not even allowed to try out and show what they could do. They were never given a chance.

It is ironic, because in 1917 and 1918 the United States sent troops to Europe to fight in World War I. President Woodrow Wilson proclaimed it "a war to make the world safe for democracy." But here at home there was no democracy in America's own national pastime.

As a result, Negro leagues sprang up in the 1920s and 1930s, consisting entirely of black players. They included Satchel Paige, the legendary pitcher who many said could be a superstar in the big leagues. And Josh Gibson, who was called the black Babe Ruth because of his tremendous home runs.

But it didn't matter how good they were. Because of prejudice, the only way they could get into a big league ballpark was by buying a ticket at the box office.

1940-1960

Jackie Robinson Breaks
the Color Barrier

DATE: April 15, 1947
OCCASION: Opening Day
PLACE: Ebbets Field, Brooklyn

For millions of Americans, baseball's most thrilling moment occurred at two o'clock that Tuesday afternoon when nine Brooklyn Dodgers sprang out of their dugout to take the field and start the 1947 baseball season. It was a memorable event in baseball history, indeed in American history. For the man who trotted to his position at first base was a broad-shouldered twenty-eight-year-old named Jack Roosevelt Robinson, and he was black.

The story of how he got there began five years earlier, in 1942, when Branch Rickey became president and general manager of the Brooklyn Dodger organization. The color barrier had disturbed Rickey for a long time, but he had never been in a position to do much about it. Now he was. In 1945, as World War II came to an end, he decided he would no longer abide by the owners' unwritten agreement that barred blacks from baseball.

Having made up his mind, Rickey searched the country for the ideal candidate to blaze the trail. He needed a black ballplayer

43

Branch Rickey in his Brooklyn Dodgers' office in April, 1947, a week before Jackie Robinson appeared in his first big league game

who was good enough to make it in the big leagues, of course, but he also wanted someone who was mature enough to take the pressure.

Whoever he was, the first black major leaguer would have to cope with taunts and insults, with name-calling and abuse. He would have to take it all and *not* retaliate. If he fought back, Rickey reasoned, those opposed to integration in baseball would be able to say, "I told you black players can't mix with whites."

The pioneer he chose was Jackie Robinson, born in Georgia in 1919 and raised in California. Formerly a baseball, football, basketball, and track star at the University of California at Los Angeles. Formerly an officer in the U.S. Army in World War II. And at the time an infielder for the Kansas City Monarchs in the Negro leagues.

Robinson was an unlikely choice. There were no doubts about

his baseball talents, but Rickey knew that he was an aggressive and highly competitive athlete who would find it difficult to accept name-calling without fighting back. However, Rickey also knew that he was extremely intelligent and would fully appreciate what was at stake.

The question was: if provoked, could Jackie control his reactions? Would he be able to keep his cool in order to pave the way for the ultimate goal—the acceptance of blacks generally into professional baseball?

Rickey asked Robinson to meet with him in his office in Brooklyn. There Rickey told him what he had in mind and the problems involved.

"I put him through the wringer that day," Rickey said many years later. "I told him he would have to curb his aggressiveness even though he would be a target for all sorts of vilification. I predicted in disgusting detail the name-calling he would have to take and warned him he would have to take it in silence and turn the other cheek. I gave him examples: suppose I'm on the opposing team in a close game and the two of us collide on a play. I swing at you and call you the worst name you can think of. What do you do?"

"You don't want a ballplayer who's afraid to fight back, do you?" asked a puzzled Jackie.

"I want a ballplayer with enough guts not to fight back," Rickey answered. "If you fight back, you'll play right into their hands. That's just what they want. You've got to do this job strictly with base hits and stolen bases and by fielding ground balls. Nothing else."

The meeting lasted three intense hours. Finally, Rickey stood in front of Robinson and asked, "Well? Do you want to do it?"

"Yes," answered Robinson. "I am not afraid to try. I'll do my best."

The provocation was all that Rickey had predicted and then some. From today's perspective, it is hard to realize the depths of racial hostility back in 1947. Today, a third of major league ballplayers are black. But not in 1947. Jackie Robinson was the first.

For that, he paid the price:

—As soon as it became known that Jackie would join the Brooklyn team, four Dodger regulars asked to be traded.

—During games, a barrage of racial insults was directed at him from fans in the grandstand and from the opposing team's bench. On several occasions, he almost lost his temper, but in each instance he remembered his promise to Branch Rickey just in time.

—A group of St. Louis Cardinals said that they would go on strike rather than play against Brooklyn if Jackie was in the line-up.

On the other hand, there were hopeful signs, too. Dodger teammates Pee Wee Reese and Eddie Stanky gave him daily support and encouragement. Once, an angry Stanky shouted at the opposing team's bench, "Why don't you guys pick on somebody who can fight back?"

St. Louis Cardinals' manager Eddie Dyer dissociated himself from some of his own players and went out of his way to wish Jackie well the first time he saw him. So did home-run slugger Hank Greenberg. Around the league, a few players on every team did the same.

Jackie Robinson on the Dodgers' bench early in the 1947 season

And Ford Frick, the president of the National League, issued a blunt ultimatum in response to the strike-threatening St. Louis Cardinals as well as to any others who might be harboring similar thoughts.

He stated: I DO NOT CARE IF HALF THE LEAGUE STRIKES. THOSE WHO DO WILL ENCOUNTER QUICK RETRIBUTION. ALL WILL BE SUSPENDED AND I DO NOT CARE IF IT WRECKS THE NATIONAL LEAGUE FOR FIVE YEARS. THIS IS THE UNITED STATES OF AMERICA AND ONE CITIZEN HAS AS MUCH RIGHT TO PLAY AS ANOTHER.

This pronouncement had such a sobering effect that within the year the worst was over and the battle virtually won. Four other black players were signed by big league teams during the 1947 season, including Larry Doby—the first in the American League—by the Cleveland Indians.

Among others, Roy Campanella joined the Dodgers in 1948, Monte Irvin the Giants in 1949, Sam Jethroe the Braves in 1950, and Willie Mays the Giants in 1951. The New York Yankees acquired their first black player, Elston Howard, in 1955. When the Boston Red Sox at long last obtained Pumpsie Green, in 1959, it finally meant that every team in the big leagues had at least one black player.

It was quite a while, however, before the first black big league manager was hired—Frank Robinson, by the Cleveland Indians, in October 1974.

Among the black players who came to the big leagues in 1948 was none other than the legendary Satchel Paige, who had been pitching in the Negro leagues since 1926. Many who had seen him in his prime claimed he was one of the greatest pitchers who ever lived, possibly the greatest. He was long past his prime, though, and it was considered a publicity stunt when the Cleveland Indians signed him on July 7, 1948, his forty-third birthday.

It was indeed good publicity because Paige quickly became the biggest box-office attraction in baseball. But it was no stunt because he just as quickly showed that he could still pitch. Perhaps not as well as ten or fifteen years earlier but well enough to surprise a lot of people.

After several successful appearances in relief, he made his first start in Cleveland on August 3 and won by a score of 5-3 before 72,000 screaming fans. Ten days later, he made his second start, this time in Chicago, and shut out the White Sox on 5 hits before a capacity crowd of 51,000. A week later, 78,000 fans in Cleveland gave him ovation after ovation as he allowed only 3 hits and won by a score of 1-0.

The legendary
Satchel Paige

Despite his age, Satchel Paige pitched in the major leagues until 1953. In 1952, at the age of forty-seven, he won 12 games (including two shutouts) and saved 10 more in relief for a next-to-last-place team that won only 64 games all season.

It has often been said that Branch Rickey signed Jackie Robinson not for idealistic reasons but because he wanted to win pennants. If so, he knew what he was doing, because Brooklyn won six pennants in the ten years Jackie was there.

Jackie Robinson

In his first season, 1947, playing under incredible tension, Jackie led the league in stolen bases and was voted Rookie of the Year. In 1949, he led the National League in hitting with a .342 batting average, led the league in stolen bases, was runner-up to the league leader in runs batted in, and was voted the league's Most Valuable Player.

But statistics alone cannot give an adequate description of what Jackie Robinson was like in a baseball game, especially a close one. Like Ty Cobb, he was dynamite on the bases, distracting opposing pitchers and infielders by taking unusually long leads, threatening to steal on almost every pitch. He successfully stole *home* 19 times, a figure exceeded by only four players in baseball history. Since he was distinctly pigeon-toed, anyone who ever saw him running the bases found it hard to forget the sight.

During the 1949 season, he gradually began to throw off the shackles that Branch Rickey had imposed on him at that famous three-hour meeting in Rickey's office. He started to talk back, to argue with umpires, to speak his mind. He felt he had fulfilled his promise to Rickey, and now he could start behaving just like anybody else.

At about the same time, the racial name-calling from opposing benches practically disappeared, no doubt because Jackie earned widespread respect for his abilities and, probably even more importantly, because black ballplayers were being signed by other teams. After all, it wouldn't be too smart for an opponent to yell a racial insult at Jackie with a black teammate sitting near him right in his own dugout.

The breaking of the color barrier was the most significant baseball event of the 1940s, but other things were also happening at the same time. As the stars of the Ruthian era slowly passed from the field of play, a new generation of ballplayers came on the scene to replace them. It was soon evident that the three most exciting were Bob Feller and Joe DiMaggio, who came to the big leagues in 1936, and Ted Williams, who arrived three years later.

Bob Feller possessed a fast ball that rivaled Walter Johnson's. Joe DiMaggio had style, courage, and leadership qualities that many say have never been equaled. And Ted Williams brought with him a superb batting eye and a striving for absolute perfection that eventually produced a .344 lifetime batting average.

Bob Feller made the most sensational debut in baseball history. An Iowa farm boy, born on November 3, 1918, he was only seven-

Joe DiMaggio, left, and Bob Feller in 1936. Joe was 21 years old and Bob only 17.

teen years old when the Cleveland Indians put him in to pitch an exhibition game against the St. Louis Cardinals in July 1936. Bob was in Cleveland on his summer vacation following his junior year in high school. He wasn't even signed to a Cleveland contract. Feller promptly struck out 8 Cardinals in only three innings, and he was on his way.

A month later, now under contract, he started his first big league game and struck out 15 batters. A few weeks later, he tied the then-existing major league record by striking out 17 batters in a game. And all before his eighteenth birthday!

A right-handed pitcher, Feller had a sizzling fast ball—it was once timed at 98.6 miles an hour—and a sharp-breaking curve. He pitched until 1956 (with four years out for military service in World War II), winning 20 or more games six times, leading the league in strikeouts seven times, and pitching 3 no-hit games. He also pitched a record *12* one-hit games.

Bob Feller set a major league record of 18 strikeouts in a nine-inning game, a feat he accomplished in 1938 at the age of nineteen. In 1946, he also set a modern record for strikeouts in a season, 348. (Rube Waddell had struck out 349 in 1904.)

Joe DiMaggio and Ted Williams were just as spectacular, each in his own way. Joltin' Joe DiMaggio's career stretched from 1936 to 1951, with three years out for military service in World War II. He batted .381 in 1939 and over .300 eleven times. Nine times he drove in over 100 runs, with a high of 167 in 1937.

In 1941, he startled the baseball world by hitting safely in 56 consecutive games, a record that appears likely to last forever.

In the outfield, DiMaggio was a picture of poetic grace. He

Joe DiMaggio during his 56-game hitting streak in 1941

never seemed to exert himself, yet he was always in the right spot to catch a dangerous line drive or a long fly ball effortlessly.

Babe Ruth and Lou Gehrig had once been the heart and soul of the New York Yankees. Now it was Joe DiMaggio. Sparked by his bat, his fielding, and, above all, his example, the Yankees won ten pennants and nine World Series in the thirteen years he patrolled center field.

A popular song of the 1940s sang his praises. Ernest Hemingway, the noted author, wrote about him in his novel *The Old Man and the Sea.* Many years after he had played his last game, Simon and Garfunkel were still yearning for his return:

> Where have you gone, Joe DiMaggio?
> A nation turns its lonely eyes on you
> What's that you say, Mrs. Robinson?
> Joltin' Joe has left and gone away

Except for Ruth and Gehrig, no player has ever been as idolized by Yankee fans as Joe DiMaggio. In the last five years of his career, when he was an inspiration to his teammates, playing with injuries that would have put anyone else on the sidelines, thunderous applause accompanied just about every move he made on the field.

A few years after his playing days were over, Joe DiMaggio was married for a time to movie star Marilyn Monroe. Marilyn was not a baseball fan, and while she certainly knew that Joe had been a famous ballplayer, it is doubtful if she ever realized *how* famous.

On one occasion, Marilyn made a special stage appearance before nearly a hundred thousand American soldiers and received a wildly cheering ovation.

"Oh, Joe," she said later that night, "it was wonderful. You've never heard such cheering!"

Joe looked at her for a moment. Very softly, he said, "Yes I have, Marilyn."

Ted Williams of the Boston Red Sox was something else again. While Joe DiMaggio did everything instinctively, as though he had been born in a baseball uniform, Ted Williams studied and practiced morning, noon, and night. More than anything, he studied and practiced hitting, and his hard work paid off. He compiled a .344 lifetime batting average, sixth highest in the twentieth century and *the* highest of anyone who has played since the 1930s.

Williams led the American League in batting six times (including a .406 batting average in 1941 and .388 in 1957), in runs batted in four times, and in home runs four times. He hit 521

Ted Williams

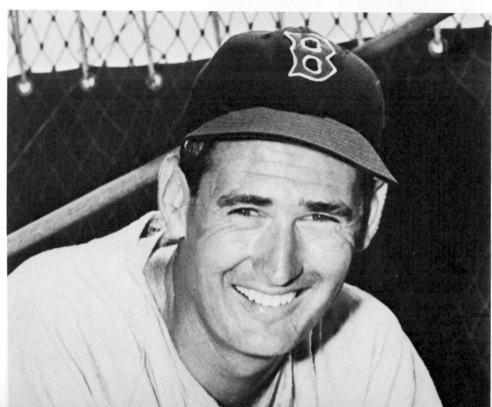

home runs during the years he played, from 1939 to 1960, even though he spent five years in the military service.

How opposing pitchers felt about seeing him come to bat is obvious. Aside from Babe Ruth, he was walked more than anyone in history—2,019 times. The Babe, by the way, received 2,056 bases on balls, only 37 more than Ted.

No one has succeeded in reaching the magic .400 batting mark since Ted Williams hit .406 in 1941. Going into the last day of the 1941 season, with a final-day double-header scheduled, his batting average was .39955. That rounds off to .400. Boston Manager Joe Cronin suggested that Ted stay out of the line-up on the closing day of the season to protect his .400 average.

"I don't want to hit .400 that way," Ted said. "If I can't really do it, I don't want it."

In the first game of the double-header he got 4 hits, and then 2 more in the second game, raising his batting average to .406.

From the start, Ted Williams was a nonconformist. He refused, for example, to wear a necktie under any circumstances. When it was announced that Joe McCarthy would become the new manager of the Boston Red Sox in 1948, the players eagerly looked forward to a confrontation between McCarthy and Williams. McCarthy was known to insist that his players always wear jackets and ties in public.

On his first morning on the job, however, Manager McCarthy showed up wearing a brightly colored sports shirt. "Any manager who can't get along with a .400 hitter," he said, "has to be out of his mind."

While Bob Feller, Joe DiMaggio, and Ted Williams were making headlines in the American League during the 1940s and

1950s, the National League was growing its own superstars.

There was Stan Musial of the St. Louis Cardinals, for instance. He batted over .300 seventeen times and finished with a .331 lifetime batting average. Musial led the league in batting seven times, and his 3,630 lifetime hits were the National League record until it was broken by Pete Rose in 1981.

And Warren Spahn, the great left-handed pitcher. Spahn won a total of 363 games, more than any left-hander in history. The only pitchers who have won more games in the twentieth century are Walter Johnson, Christy Mathewson, and Grover Cleveland Alexander. Spahn won 20 or more games thirteen times for the Boston and then the Milwaukee Braves, including 2 no-hitters.

In addition, four newcomers arrived in the National League in the 1950s who obviously had bright futures. Their names were Sandy Koufax, Willie Mays, Hank Aaron, and Roberto Clemente. A Jew, two blacks, and a Puerto Rican. Times certainly had changed.

Stan Musial: a .331 lifetime batting average over 22 years

>>

MODERN TIMES

"Isn't It Great Just To Be Here!"

Here's a riddle: how come pitcher Sandy Koufax joined the Brooklyn Dodgers in 1955, was never traded, yet played most of his career in Los Angeles?

The answer, of course, is that in 1958 the Brooklyn Dodgers moved from the East Coast to the West Coast and became the Los Angeles Dodgers.

For half a century, from 1903 through 1952, the geographic distribution of major league teams remained unaltered. During all of those years, the National and American leagues were organized as follows:

NATIONAL LEAGUE	AMERICAN LEAGUE
Boston Braves	Boston Red Sox
Chicago Cubs	Chicago White Sox
New York Giants	New York Yankees
Philadelphia Phillies	Philadelphia Athletics
St. Louis Cardinals	St. Louis Browns
Brooklyn Dodgers	Cleveland Indians
Cincinnati Reds	Detroit Tigers
Pittsburgh Pirates	Washington Senators

The first change in fifty years occurred in 1953 when the Boston Braves moved to Milwaukee and became the Milwaukee Braves. That started a game of musical chairs.

In 1954, the St. Louis Browns moved to Baltimore and turned into the Baltimore Orioles. In 1955, the Philadelphia Athletics transferred to Kansas City. In 1958, the Giants moved from New York to San Francisco and the Dodgers from Brooklyn to Los Angeles.

In 1966, the Braves moved again, this time from Milwaukee to Atlanta. In 1968, so did the Athletics, this time from Kansas City to Oakland. That left Milwaukee and Kansas City without big league baseball teams, just as they had been before the Braves and Athletics arrived in the first place.

Shibe Park, formerly the home of the Philadelphia Athletics, in 1974

In the 1960s, both leagues expanded from eight to twelve teams. The National League added the Houston Astros and New York Mets in 1962 and the Montreal Expos and San Diego Padres in 1969. The American League added the California Angels and Minnesota Twins in 1961 and the Seattle Pilots and Kansas City Royals in 1969.

Now Kansas City had a major league team again, but not Milwaukee. However, after only one year in Seattle, the Pilots moved to Milwaukee and turned into the Milwaukee Brewers. This gave Milwaukee a team once more but left Seattle out in the cold.

In 1972, the American League's Washington Senators moved to Texas to become the Texas Rangers, and in 1977 the league expanded from twelve to fourteen teams by adding the Toronto Blue Jays and the Seattle Mariners. So Seattle had a team again, but Washington didn't.

The transfer of teams from one city to another was motivated by money. Owners of teams losing money moved to where they thought they could make money. Owners of teams making money moved to where they thought they could make even more. Sometimes they thought wrong, so they moved again.

Long-distance airplane travel made it all possible. Until the early 1950s, all the major league cities were concentrated on the East Coast or in the nearby Midwest, within overnight railroad distance from each other. St. Louis was the farthest west, less than a third of the way across the country from the East Coast.

Teams traveled by train, and trains are too slow to cross the entire country in a few hours. When regular, reliable, safe, and swift cross-continental airplane service began, in the late 1940s, it was only a matter of time before teams would become more widely scattered geographically.

Not all the players were happy about the shift from trains to planes. Planes were a relatively new form of travel then, and trips were often bumpy and nerve-racking. Even today, many players are nervous when they have to fly, which is often as much as three times a week.

Boston Red Sox outfielder Jackie Jensen decided to retire early because of his fear of flying. Dodger pitcher Don Newcombe tried self-hypnosis to overcome similar fears, with only limited success.

Dodger shortstop Pee Wee Reese once tried to calm pitcher Kirby Higbe. "When your number's up, you'll go," Reese said. "It doesn't matter if you're up here or on the ground."

But that didn't satisfy Higbe. "Suppose I'm up here with some pilot," Higbe moaned, "and my number isn't up, but *his* is!"

Some owners of teams that were losing money made a valiant attempt to stay put by attracting more fans at the box office. Bill Veeck, the owner of the St. Louis Browns, for example, got nationwide headlines when he went so far as to sign a 26-year-old midget as a pinch-hitter. Veeck figured he was a cinch to get a base on balls, and if he was put in to pinch-hit when the bases were loaded, that could force in the winning run.

The midget's name was Eddie Gaedel, and he was 3 feet 7 inches tall and weighed 65 pounds. The number on the back of his uniform was 1/8.

St. Louis Manager Zack Taylor put him in to pinch-hit in a game against the Detroit Tigers on August 19, 1951. As expected, Gaedel walked on four straight pitches, all of which were high. The next day, however, the American League banned further use

Eddie Gaedel at bat on August 19, 1951. Bob Swift is the catcher and Ed Hurley the umpire.

of Gaedel on the grounds that it was a publicity stunt detrimental to baseball.

With the departure of the Dodgers and Giants to the West Coast in 1958, New York area fans lost two of the greatest stars of all time: Sandy Koufax and Willie Mays.

Sandy Koufax grew up in Brooklyn and joined the Dodgers in 1955 at the age of nineteen. A left-handed pitcher, for many years he had blinding speed and a good curve but no control. When he finally put it all together, in 1962, he became the best pitcher of his generation.

Koufax won 25 games for the Los Angeles Dodgers in 1963, 26 in 1965, and 27 in 1966. Twice he struck out 18 batters in a game, tying the record Feller had set in 1938. He pitched a then-

Sandy Koufax

record 4 no-hit games and was voted the best pitcher in both leagues in 1963, 1965, and 1966.

But it ended as quickly as it had begun. In November 1966, after his best season ever and not yet thirty-one years old, Sandy Koufax announced that he would never pitch again.

A severe case of arthritis had developed in his left elbow. Before pitching, he had to be given injections, during a game his arm would swell up, and afterward his elbow had to be packed in ice. Doctors warned that if he continued pitching, he would risk serious permanent injury. So at the peak of his career, Sandy was forced to retire.

Willie Mays, on the other hand, seemed to go on forever. He came to the New York Giants in 1951 at the age of twenty and didn't stop playing until 1973. In between, he hit 660 home runs, more than anyone except Hank Aaron and Babe Ruth, stole over 300 bases, and batted over .300 ten times.

In center field, he made acrobatic catches and threw runners out as though he had a rifle for an arm. Some veteran baseball writers believe that Willie Mays' all-around accomplishments at bat, on the bases, and in the outfield were so exceptional that he deserves to be called the greatest baseball player who ever lived—even greater than Babe Ruth, Ty Cobb, Honus Wagner, or Joe DiMaggio.

When they were both playing center field in New York, arguments arose constantly over who was better: Willie Mays of the Giants or Mickey Mantle of the Yankees. Mantle had more raw speed and sheer power than Mays—he had more raw speed and

Willie Mays

sheer power than *anybody*—but injuries hampered him throughout his career.

A switch-hitter, Mantle hit 536 lifetime home runs, 373 batting
left-handed and 163 batting right-handed. From either side, his
home runs traveled prodigious distances. In terms of how high
and how far they went, he was in a class with Babe Ruth, Jimmie
Foxx, and the Negro leagues' fabled Josh Gibson.

Mantle led the American League in home runs four times, with
peaks of 52 in 1956 and 54 in 1961. His 54 in 1961, however,
failed to lead the league because that was the year Yankee teammate Roger Maris startled the country by breaking Babe Ruth's
famous record of 60 home runs in a season.

Roger Maris has just hit home run number 61, breaking
Babe Ruth's record.

Poor Roger Maris! He never received the recognition he de-
served for breaking baseball's best-known record. One reason is
that he did it in the then-brand-new 162-game season, while the
Babe hit his 60 homers in the shorter 154-game schedule that
had previously existed. After 154 games in 1961, Maris had
"only" 59 home runs.

In addition, many people resented *anyone* surpassing *anything* Babe Ruth did. As Maris got closer and closer to number
60, he was booed more than he was cheered. The booing con-
fused and upset him so much he could hardly sleep at night. He
got so tired, cranky, and nervous that his hair even started falling
out.

Nevertheless, he refused to give up. He finally hit number 60
and tied Babe Ruth's record with four games left to play. And
then, in the final game of the season, his last chance, in the

fourth inning, he launched a dramatic drive into the right-field seats at Yankee Stadium for home run number 61, a record that still stands. If his record lasts as long as Babe Ruth's did, it won't be broken until 1995.

After Maris broke the Babe's single-season home-run record in 1961, other records that everyone thought were indestructible also started falling like trees in a hurricane:

—In 1962, the Dodgers' Maury Wills broke Ty Cobb's 1915 record of 96 stolen bases in a season by stealing 104 bases. Only twelve years later, Lou Brock stole 118, and then Rickey Henderson reached 130 in 1982.

—In 1965, Sandy Koufax set a single-season strikeout record by fanning 382 batters. And only eight years later, Nolan Ryan overtook him with 383.

—As the 1960s began, only two men in history had pitched as many as 3 no-hit games: Cy Young and Bob Feller. But then Sandy Koufax pitched 4 no-hitters, followed by Nolan Ryan who went him one better with 5.

—On April 8, 1974, the Atlanta Braves' Hank Aaron broke Babe Ruth's record of 714 lifetime home runs by hitting his 715th homer. Aaron retired in 1976 with a record 755 home runs. (The legend of Babe Ruth is hard to overcome. Soon after he hit number 715, two books came out about the life of Hank Aaron, but four books came out about the life of Babe Ruth!)

—In 1977, the Cardinals' Lou Brock broke Ty Cobb's record of 892 lifetime stolen bases by stealing his 893rd base. Brock retired in 1979 with a record 938 stolen bases.

(left)
Lou Brock: 938 life-
time stolen bases

(right)
Rickey Henderson.
His 130 stolen
bases in 1982 set a
new single-season
record.

In 1947, Jackie Robinson was the first black ballplayer to be allowed in the major leagues. One often-heard defense of the pre-1947 color ban was that black ballplayers couldn't play up to big league standards, so it was best not to hire them to begin with. Hank Aaron was thirteen years of age in 1947, Lou Brock eight years old. As Jackie Robinson trotted out to his position on Opening Day that year, who could have imagined that these two black youngsters would someday break the records of baseball's most illustrious heroes, Babe Ruth and Ty Cobb?

Hank Aaron was born in 1934 in Mobile, Alabama. He broke into the major leagues with Milwaukee in 1954, but it was three years before he hit as many as 30 home runs in one season. Once he started, however, he didn't stop. In fourteen of the next sixteen years, he hit between 30 and 45 homers a year.

Aaron ended the 1973 season with 713, just one short of Ruth's record. With pressure building up all winter, he nevertheless tied the record with the *very first* swing of his bat in 1974. Such total and complete concentration is almost superhuman. And four days later, before a Monday night nationwide television audience, he hit record-breaking home run number 715 over the left-field fence in Atlanta.

Lou Brock grew up in Collinston, Louisiana, one of nine children in a poor rural family. One day in school, he created a disturbance in class and as punishment was sent to the school library.

"The teacher told me to look up five baseball players," he recalled years later. "They were Jackie Robinson, Joe DiMaggio, Don Newcombe, Roy Campanella, and Stan Musial. I still remember them. Then I was to stand in front of the class and give a report on what I'd read. That's how I started to get interested in baseball."

Brock made it to Southern University at Baton Rouge, Louisiana, where he was a mathematics major until a $30,000 bonus persuaded him to leave college after his junior year for a baseball career. For twelve consecutive years, from 1965 through 1976, he stole over 50 bases a season, reaching his peak with a record-shattering 118 in 1974.

Lou Brock represented a return to the old-fashioned style of baseball—bunting, base stealing, trying to outthink the opposition—that had almost disappeared between 1920 and the late 1960s. Home runs dominated the game during those years. But the geographic expansion of the major leagues in the 1960s meant the construction of many new ballparks, a number of which were built with artificial turf on the playing field instead of real grass.

The ball behaves differently on artificial turf. Ground balls skip through the infield faster because synthetic turf is smoother than grass. Also, the ball usually bounces higher because artificial turf is laid, like a rug, on a fairly hard surface. Running speed became more important for outfielders so they could get to a line drive and cut it off before it skipped between them and rolled all the way to the fence for a triple or an inside-the-park home run.

Swinging for distance did not disappear, but an increasing number of players also began to concentrate on skills that had been neglected since the early 1920s.

It was no accident, then, that three of the brightest stars of the 1960s and 1970s—Roberto Clemente, Rod Carew, and Pete

Roberto Clemente

Rose—played the way ballplayers used to play in the early days of baseball.

Roberto Clemente was born in Carolina, Puerto Rico. A proud, moody, and as he grew older, deeply caring man, he joined the Pittsburgh Pirates in 1955 and four times thereafter led the league in batting. He specialized in line-drive doubles and triples, where his speed was crucial, although he hit home runs from time to time as well.

He hit over .300 thirteen times, over .350 three times. In right field, his throwing arm was recognized as the strongest and most accurate in baseball.

On September 30, 1972, Clemente got his 3,000th major league hit, something only ten players had accomplished before him. Tragically, it would be his last regular-season hit in the big leagues. Because three months later, on New Year's Eve, a nervous Roberto Clemente—he never did like to fly—climbed into a rickety old plane along with a pilot and three others and took off from San Juan, Puerto Rico. The plane was loaded with eight tons of desperately needed food, clothing, and medical supplies that Roberto Clemente was personally delivering to Managua, Nicaragua, which had been devastated by an earthquake a week earlier.

The airplane never made it to Nicaragua. It practically never made it off the ground. One engine exploded immediately after takeoff, followed by further explosions, and it plunged into the ocean barely a mile off the Puerto Rican coast. There were no survivors.

From a poverty-stricken boyhood, Roberto Clemente rose to wealth and fame. But he never forgot his roots, and he tried to use his money and prestige to benefit others as well as himself. He died on a mission of mercy, trying to help people in need, which is the same way he had lived.

Rodney Cline Carew was born in Panama in 1945. He was named Rodney Cline—not the most common Panamanian name—after Dr. Rodney Cline, an American doctor who luckily happened to be nearby and helped deliver him when his mother unexpectedly gave birth while on her way to the hospital.

Carew joined the Minnesota Twins in 1967. Like Clemente, his counterpart in the National League, he specialized in line-drive doubles and triples. Rod Carew led the league in batting seven times, tying him with Rogers Hornsby and Stan Musial. Only Ty Cobb and Honus Wagner have won more batting championships.

Roberto Clemente, for all his doubles and triples, also hit 240 home runs. Although Carew has over 2,500 big league hits, less than a hundred have been home runs. He is a true throwback to the early days of baseball.

As is Pete Rose, probably the most exciting ballplayer of his time. By combining the single-minded determination of Ty Cobb with the joy and flair of Willie Mays, Pete Rose symbolizes the underlying unity of baseball from the early days to the present.

Playing with the Cincinnati Reds and then the Philadelphia Phillies, he has led the National League in batting three times, in doubles five times, and in hits six times. Once, in 1978, he even hit 3 home runs in one game.

Born in Cincinnati in 1941, Pete Rose has always played every game as though he were a rookie trying to make the team. In 1978, he hit in 44 consecutive games, the only player to have

Pete Rose

challenged seriously the record 56-game hitting streak set by Joe DiMaggio in 1941.

Only three players have hit in more than 40 consecutive games in the twentieth century: George Sisler (41) in 1922, Pete Rose (44) in 1978, and, of course, DiMaggio (56) in 1941.

In 1981, Rose got hit number 3,631, thereby passing Stan Musial as the National League's all-time leader in hits. At the end of the 1981 season, only two players in all of baseball history had more lifetime hits than Pete Rose—Hank Aaron with 3,771 hits and Ty Cobb with 4,191. During 1982, Pete got hit number 3,772 and passed Aaron. Now there's only Ty Cobb ahead of him!

The glory of Pete Rose emerged in the famous sixth game of the 1975 World Series between Pete's Cincinnati Reds and the Boston Red Sox, a game that many say was the most exciting World Series game ever played. Cincinnati was leading in the series three games to two, and Boston had to win to stay alive.

In the very first inning, Boston jumped ahead, 3-0. But the Reds tied it up in the fifth inning and then went ahead in the top half of the eighth, 6-3. It looked like it was all over for Boston.

In the bottom half of the eighth inning, however, with two outs, Boston's Bernie Carbo pinch-hit a 3-run homer, and suddenly the game was all tied up again, 6-6.

Boston then loaded the bases in the bottom of the ninth, but Cincinnati left fielder George Foster threw Boston's Denny Doyle out at home plate to prevent the winning run from scoring.

In the eleventh inning, Cincinnati second baseman Joe Morgan smashed what looked like a sure home run, but Boston right fielder Dwight Evans made a sensational catch to keep the score tied.

Finally, in the twelfth inning, Boston catcher Carlton Fisk won the game for the Red Sox, 7-6, with a dramatic home run that bounced high off the left-field foul pole.

An inning earlier, in the eleventh inning of this thriller, Pete Rose came to home plate for what—although he didn't know it then—would be his last time at bat in the game. As he stepped into the batter's box, he turned to Boston catcher Carlton Fisk and home-plate umpire Satch Davidson and grinned in delight.

"Hey, I don't know who's going to win this," he said, "but isn't it great just to be here!"

>>

PART TWO

>>

Hank Aaron hitting record-breaking home run number 715
on April 8, 1974. The ball is a blur as it leaves the bat.

BATTING

"You Just Keep Your Eye
on the Ball"

Did you ever think about how difficult it must be to hit a baseball thrown by a major league pitcher?

An average big league fast ball travels at a speed of almost 90 miles an hour. The distance from the pitcher's mound to home plate is 60 feet 6 inches. But since the pitcher takes a stride when throwing it, the ball is actually released from a distance of only about 55 feet. At 90 miles an hour, the ball reaches home plate in *four-tenths of a second.*

However, the batter can't wait until the ball reaches home plate to decide whether or not to swing at it. By then it's too late. He has to make up his mind *before* it arrives, deciding what to do when it is about 15 feet away. This gives him only *three-tenths of a second* in which to judge the pitch, decide whether or not to swing (or to duck!), and to start moving his bat to make contact.

Only three-tenths of a second! And that's for an average 90-mile-an-hour fast ball. Bob Feller's fast ball was timed at 98.6 miles an hour and Nolan Ryan's at 100.9 miles an hour.

No wonder only *eleven* men in the twentieth century have been able to hit safely as often as 34 percent of the time—that is, have a lifetime batting average as high as .340.

Here are the eleven, along with their lifetime batting averages:

Ty Cobb	.367	Babe Ruth	.342
Rogers Hornsby	.358	Harry Heilmann	.342
Joe Jackson	.356	Bill Terry	.341
Lefty O'Doul	.349	George Sisler	.340
Tris Speaker	.345	Lou Gehrig	.340
Ted Williams	.344		

Even these hitters—the eleven best in the twentieth century—*failed* to hit safely almost two-thirds of the time. Ty Cobb's .367 batting average means he hit safely 36.7 percent of the time, so he must have failed to do so 63.3 percent of the time.

George Sisler and Lou Gehrig hit .340, which means they hit safely 34 percent of the time and failed to get a hit 66 percent of the time.

A .300 hitter—the traditional standard of excellence in bat-

Tris Speaker. He had a .345 lifetime batting average from 1908 through 1928, and was considered the greatest defensive center fielder of his time.

ting—succeeds in hitting safely only 30 percent of the time and fails in his turn at bat 70 percent of the time.

A player's batting average is the number of hits he gets divided by the number of times at bat, carried out to three decimal places. Every single, double, triple, and home run counts as just one hit. If a batter got a hit every time he came to bat, his batting average would be 1.000 (called batting a thousand). A player who has come to bat but has no hits at all is batting .000 (called batting zero).

In 1973, Rod Carew got 203 hits in 580 times at bat to lead the American League with a batting average of .350 (called simply three fifty). He hit safely exactly 35 percent of the time.

In 1976, George Brett got 215 hits in 645 times at bat to lead the league with a batting average of .333 (three thirty-three). He hit safely exactly one-third of the time.

When calculating batting averages, bases on balls do not count as times at bat, so they don't affect a player's batting average. However, if a batter gets on base because of an opposing player's fielding error, it does count as a time at bat—and since it isn't a hit, his batting average falls.

Of the eleven .340-or-better hitters just listed, nine batted left-handed and only two batted right-handed (Hornsby and Heilmann). That is not as surprising as it looks.

Left-handed batters have advantages over right-handed batters. The most obvious advantage is that they end their swing two steps closer to first base and are already moving toward first base as they finish swinging. These two steps are important in beating out ground balls to the infield. Right-handed batters finish swinging with their momentum carrying them toward *third* base, and they also have to take those two extra steps in running to first base.

Another advantage left-handed batters have is that they usually hit right-handed pitchers better than they hit left-handed pitchers, and 70 percent of major league pitchers are right-handed. On the other hand, right-handed batters usually hit lefties better than righties, but only 30 percent of big league pitchers are lefties.

Because of this fact—*left-handed batters hit righties best, while right-handed batters hit lefties best*—when a manager puts a pinch-hitter into a game, the pinch-hitter will almost always be a left-handed batter if the pitcher is righty and a right-handed batter if the pitcher is lefty.

For the same reason, except it's the other side of the coin, when a relief pitcher is called into a game, he will almost always be a lefty if a left-handed batter is up next and a righty if a right-handed batter is up next.

Why is it that left-handed batters hit righties best and right-handed batters hit lefties best?

The main reason is that a typical curve ball naturally curves *away* from the side it is thrown from. This is because of how it is thrown and the way it spins. A curve ball thrown by a right-handed pitcher curves *away* from a right-handed batter and *toward* a left-handed batter. This helps the left-handed batter because *it seems to be easier to judge and to hit a ball curving toward you* as compared with one curving away from you.

Similarly, a curve ball thrown by a lefty curves away from a left-handed batter and *toward* a right-handed batter, giving right-handed batters an advantage.

Just to make things more complicated, a few pitchers throw a screwball—like Christy Mathewson, Carl Hubbell, Tug McGraw, and Fernando Valenzuela, to name only four.

A screwball is a *reverse curve,* so things work just the opposite. Thrown by a right-handed pitcher like Mathewson, a screwball curves *toward* a right-handed batter and is thus easier for him to hit than it is for a left-handed batter to hit. Thrown by a left-handed pitcher like Hubbell, McGraw, or Valenzuela, a screwball curves toward a left-handed batter.

Since left-handed batters hit righties best, while right-handed batters hit lefties best—except when the pitcher has a good screwball—there are obvious advantages to being a switch-hitter. A switch-hitter bats left-handed when facing right-handed pitchers and turns around and bats right-handed when facing left-handed pitchers. Pete Rose and Mickey Mantle are the two best-known and most successful switch-hitters in recent baseball history.

A switch-hitter, however, has to keep his wits about him. Honus Wagner was fond of telling the story of Jimmy St. Vrain, a pitcher for the Chicago Cubs in the early 1900s. Jimmy, who normally batted right-handed, was a terrible hitter. To see if he might possibly do better from the other side of the plate, he tried batting left-handed one day in a game against Honus Wagner's Pittsburgh Pirates.

On the very first pitch, St. Vrain tapped a slow ground ball to Wagner at shortstop and took off as fast as he could go, but he was turned around and on the opposite side of the plate from where he was used to batting, and instead of running to first base he took off for *third!*

Everyone in the ballpark watched in astonishment as Jimmy

raced to third base, head down, spikes flying, determined to get there ahead of the throw. And Wagner, after fielding the ball, wasn't sure what to do with it himself.

"I'm standing there with the ball in my hand," Wagner said later, "looking at this guy running from home to third, and for an instant I didn't know *where* to throw it. When I finally did throw to first base, I wasn't at all sure it was the right thing to do."

In general, batters fall into one of two categories: they are either mainly *place hitters* or mainly *power hitters*. A few are

Rod Carew

both, depending on what they want to do when they come to bat, but most are primarily one or the other.

Place hitters try to slap the ball through or over the infield, trying mostly for singles and doubles and an occasional longer hit. Power hitters aim for distance, swinging for the fences and settling for less when they have to.

Here are the top power hitters of all time, the twelve men who have hit 500 or more lifetime home runs, along with the number of home runs each has hit. Their career batting averages are in parentheses:

Hank Aaron	755	(.305)	Jimmie Foxx	534	(.325)
Babe Ruth	714	(.342)	Willie McCovey	521	(.270)
Willie Mays	660	(.302)	Ted Williams	521	(.344)
Frank Robinson	586	(.294)	Ernie Banks	512	(.274)
Harmon Killebrew	573	(.256)	Eddie Mathews	512	(.271)
Mickey Mantle	536	(.298)	Mel Ott	511	(.304)

Only Babe Ruth and Ted Williams are among the leaders in home runs *and* among the top eleven in batting average. Since power hitters swing from the heels trying to hit the ball as far as they can, their batting average usually suffers.

Almost all the old-timers who played before 1920—before Babe Ruth and the lively ball—were strictly place hitters. However, all those who have played since then are not necessarily power hitters. A quick way to classify someone as a place hitter or a power hitter is by *the percentage of his hits that are home runs.*

Of Ty Cobb's 4,191 lifetime hits, only 118, or 3 percent, were home runs. In recent years, throwbacks to the strictly place hitters of the old days—like Rod Carew and Pete Rose—still special-

Mickey Mantle
waiting his turn
at bat

Mantle hit 536
career home
runs and also
struck out (as
below) 1,710
times.

ize in poking the ball between the infielders and spraying line drives all over the field. Only 3 percent of Rod Carew's hits and 4 percent of Pete Rose's are homers.

At the other extreme are free-swinging strictly power hitters like Dave Kingman, Harmon Killebrew, and Mike Schmidt. *Between 25 and 30 percent* of their hits are home runs. If they connect safely, chances are better than one out of four that the ball will go out of the park.

Most players are somewhere in between these two extremes, but they generally tend to be close to one end of the scale or the other. In other words, relatively few are in the middle, ready to do either as the occasion warrants, with about 13–17 percent of their hits being home runs.

Here are fifteen well-known ballplayers along with the percentage of their hits that are home runs. Those in the first column are extreme power hitters, those in the third column are extreme place hitters. Those in the middle go either way, depending on the circumstances when they come to bat:

Dave Kingman	29%	Joe DiMaggio	16%	Pete Rose	4%
Harmon Killebrew	27%	Carlton Fisk	15%	Rod Carew	3%
Mike Schmidt	26%	Carl Yastrzemski	13%	Ty Cobb	3%
Ralph Kiner	25%	Al Kaline	13%	Joe Sewell	2%
Babe Ruth	25%	Stan Musial	13%	Lloyd Waner	1%

A lot of mainly (but not extreme) power hitters are around the 20 percent mark—about 20 percent of their hits are home runs—like Mickey Mantle, Reggie Jackson, Willie Mays, Hank Aaron, Jimmie Foxx, and Ted Williams.

A lot of mainly (but not extreme) place hitters are around the 10 percent level—about 10 percent of their hits are home runs—

like Steve Garvey, Rogers Hornsby, Thurman Munson, Jackie Robinson, Roberto Clemente, and George Brett.

It isn't necessarily better to be a power hitter or a place hitter provided you're good at whatever you are. After all, Babe Ruth is in the first column, Joe DiMaggio is in the second, and Ty Cobb is in the third. Each is a different kind of hitter, but each has a claim to being one of the greatest of all time.

Although it isn't necessarily better to be one rather than the other, there are definite differences among them. Except for Babe Ruth, Ted Williams, and Jimmie Foxx, power hitters have lower batting averages than the others. On the other hand, extreme place hitters have higher batting averages.

However, it's the power hitters who drive in the runs. Harmon Killebrew batted in 100 or more runs nine times and Ralph Kiner six times. Among the place hitters in the third column, Pete Rose and Lloyd Waner never did have as many as 100 runs batted in, and Rod Carew managed it only once.

Power hitters have one failing they cannot seem to control: they strike out a lot. Dave Kingman, in the first column, strikes out once out of every 3 times he comes to bat; Mike Schmidt, once out of every 4 times; Harmon Killebrew, once in every 5 times; Babe Ruth, once in every 6 times; and Ralph Kiner, once in every 7 times.

Compare that with the extreme place hitters. Ty Cobb struck out once in every 32 times he came to bat, Lloyd Waner once out of every 45 times, and Joe Sewell once out of every 63 times he came to bat over a fourteen-year career.

Indeed, Joe Sewell was the toughest man to strike out in baseball history. Shortstop for the Cleveland Indians from 1920 to

(left)
Ralph Kiner, one of the top home run hitters of all time. On average, Kiner hit a home run every 14.1 times at bat, a frequency exceeded only by Babe Ruth, who homered on average once every 11.8 times at bat.

(right)
Mike Schmidt, the leading home run hitter of the late 1970s and early 1980s

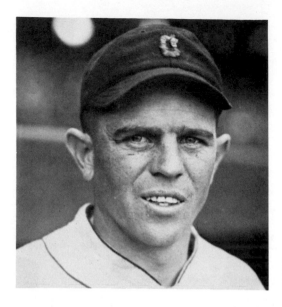

Joe Sewell, the hardest man to strike out in baseball history

1928 and third baseman for the Indians and the New York Yankees from 1929 to 1933, he compiled a .312 lifetime batting average as he came to bat a total of 7,132 times and struck out only 114 times. In 1925, he batted 608 times and struck out on only four occasions.

Those who seek advice from the experts so they can learn the secret of success are frequently doomed to disappointment. The experts often do things so naturally, like tying one's shoelaces, that they have trouble explaining it to others. A teammate once asked Joe Sewell the secret of how he avoided striking out.

Sewell stammered, not sure what to say. "Well," he finally answered, trying to be helpful, "you just keep your eye on the ball."

Easier said than done when it's coming toward you at 90 miles an hour and you've got only three-tenths of a second to make your move!

PITCHING

"I Lost My Fast Ball"

Connie Mack, who managed in the big leagues for fifty years (yes, fifty years!), used to say that pitching is 75 percent of baseball. Other experts have put the figure even higher, some as high as 90 percent. While that might be going too far, it is generally agreed that good hitting by itself cannot win pennants but that good pitching can.

In 1930, for example, the Philadelphia Phillies had a *team* batting average of .315. They scored an average of 6 runs a game. But they allowed the opposition an average of 8 runs a game and finished in last place. In 1947, the New York Giants hit a record 221 home runs and couldn't finish any higher than fourth.

On the other hand, the 1965 Los Angeles Dodgers had a team batting average of .245 and hit only 78 home runs all year. But with Sandy Koufax and Don Drysdale pitching, they won both the pennant and the World Series.

It is also generally agreed that good pitchers can usually stop good hitters. Ted Williams often said that hitting a baseball properly is the single most difficult thing to do in all of sports. If so, pitching a baseball properly must be the second most difficult thing.

Only eight pitchers in the twentieth century have managed to win as many as 300 games. Here are the eight and their lifetime victory totals:

Walter Johnson	416	Eddie Plank	327
Grover Cleveland Alexander	373	Gaylord Perry	307
Christy Mathewson	373	Lefty Grove	300
Warren Spahn	363	Early Wynn	300

One pitcher in history *did* win more games than Walter Johnson—Cy Young, who won 511. The annual award for the best pitcher in each league is named after him. However, he won over half his games before 1900.

Some others who might have won 300 games were unfortunately prevented from doing so by things outside their control. Bob Feller, for instance, won 266 games. However, he was in the military service almost four years during World War II, when he was at the peak of his career.

The year before he left, he won 25 games, and the year he returned he won 26. If he had won just 20 games a season the four years he was gone, he would have ended his career fifth on the all-time list, right behind Warren Spahn.

And imagine how many games Sandy Koufax might have won if he hadn't been forced to retire before his thirty-first birthday because of arthritis. Even so, he still won 165 games, 111 of them in his last five years.

In that five-year period, 1962 through 1966, Koufax had an *earned run average* (ERA) of 1.95, which means he allowed the opposition an average of slightly less than 2 earned runs a game.

The number of games a pitcher wins is affected not only by

(left)
Warren Spahn, a
lifetime 363-game
winner

(right)
Sandy Koufax

how well he pitches but also by what his teammates do—for example, whether or not they get him any runs. For that reason, the best measure of a pitcher's ability is his ERA. This is the average number of earned runs he allows the opposition over nine innings.

For purposes of figuring a pitcher's ERA, "unearned" runs are separated from "earned" runs, although one kind of run is just as good as another when it comes to winning a ball game. An unearned run is one that is due to a fielding error, so it isn't really the pitcher's fault.

A pitcher's ERA is calculated as the number of earned runs he allows divided by the number of innings he pitched. The result is the average number of earned runs allowed in an inning. This figure is then multiplied by 9 in order to convert it to nine innings. In that way, it gives the average number of earned runs allowed in a nine-inning game. The final figure is carried out to two decimal places.

An easier way to do the exact same thing is to simply multiply a pitcher's earned runs by 9 and divide the result by the number of innings pitched. If a pitcher allows 10 earned runs in 45 innings, for example, multiply 10 by 9 = 90 and divide by 45 = 2.00. On average, the pitcher has allowed exactly 2 earned runs a game.

In 1980, Pat Zachry of the New York Mets allowed 55 earned runs in 165 innings. Multiply 55 by 9 = 495 and divide by 165 = 3.00. Pat Zachry allowed the opposition an average of exactly 3 earned runs a game in 1980.

Or take Fernando Valenzuela: in 1981, when he won the Cy Young Award as the best pitcher in the National League, he allowed 53 earned runs in 192 innings. Multiply 53 by 9 = 477 and divide by 192 = 2.48. Fernando allowed the opposition slightly less than 2½ earned runs a game in 1981.

An ERA under 3.00 is considered excellent, and one under 2.00 is fantastic.

In order to see how remarkable Sandy Koufax's 1.95 ERA was for the five years from 1962 through 1966, here are twenty great pitchers and the ERA of each *for the five consecutive years during each pitcher's career when his ERA was lowest.* All of the 300-game winners are included, plus twelve more all-time superstars:

Walter Johnson	1.49	Carl Hubbell	2.40
Grover C. Alexander	1.64	Gaylord Perry	2.55
Christy Mathewson	1.69	Lefty Grove	2.56
Sandy Koufax	1.95	Bob Feller	2.68
Eddie Plank	2.05	Dazzy Vance	2.76
Babe Ruth	2.16	Steve Carlton	2.77
Juan Marichal	2.30	Warren Spahn	2.87
Tom Seaver	2.35	Nolan Ryan	2.94
Jim Palmer	2.35	Dizzy Dean	2.95
Bob Gibson	2.35	Early Wynn	3.01

Some pitchers from every era are included in the twenty. Except for Sandy Koufax, the first six pitched with the dead ball—that is, before 1920—which helps account for their very low ERAs.

Carl Hubbell, Lefty Grove, Dazzy Vance, and Dizzy Dean are the cream of the 1920s and 1930s.

Bob Feller, Warren Spahn, and Early Wynn were among the best in the 1940s and 1950s.

Bob Feller

Sandy Koufax, Juan Marichal, and Bob Gibson were baseball's top pitchers in the 1960s, as were Tom Seaver, Jim Palmer, Gaylord Perry, Steve Carlton, and Nolan Ryan in the 1970s.

Koufax's five-year ERA of 1.95 is the best since the lively ball was introduced in 1920. Indeed, it is one of the best five-year pitching records in the entire twentieth century, regardless of the ball being lively or dead.

Babe Ruth, by the way, seems to pop up everywhere. He is near the top of every list, whether it involves batting average, home runs, or pitching excellence.

Of the twenty great pitchers listed, thirteen are right-handers and seven left-handers. The seven lefties are Sandy Koufax, Eddie Plank, Babe Ruth, Carl Hubbell, Lefty Grove, Steve Carlton, and Warren Spahn. This is roughly what might be expected, since about 70 percent of major league pitchers are right-handers.

Babe Ruth
as a left-handed
pitcher with the
Boston Red Sox
in 1916

Juan Marichal

One advantage that lefties have over righties is in holding base runners close to first base. A left-handed pitcher is facing first base when he takes his pitching position, so it is easier for him to keep a man on first from taking too big a lead than it is for a right-handed pitcher, who is facing in the opposite direction.

Sam Jones, a star pitcher in the American League from 1914 to 1935, attributed his long career to the fact that he rarely threw to first base to hold base runners close. He claimed that there were only so many pitches in his arm, and he didn't believe in wasting them by throwing to first base.

"What you do instead of throwing," he later told a friend, "is look at the guy on first base. That's all, just stand there on the pitching mound and look at him. There's no need to throw. If you stare at him long enough, it'll get to be too much for him, and he'll lean back toward the base. *Then* you pitch. There was a time there, for five years, I never once threw to first base to chase a runner back. Not one time in five years. Ripley even put it in *Believe It or Not*. Then one day, to everybody's surprise, I *did* it. I threw to first base. Had the guy out by a mile. But it didn't do any good. The man was safe because my first baseman was as surprised as anyone, and he dropped the ball!"

Just as some batters are mainly power hitters, some pitchers are mainly power pitchers. There are very few of them, however. The few who are mainly power pitchers rely primarily on their blazing speed. To get away with it, their fast ball has to reach at least 90–95 miles an hour regularly and consistently.

Included in that small elite group are Walter Johnson, Dazzy Vance, Lefty Grove, Bob Feller, Sandy Koufax, and Nolan Ryan.

They simply overpower batters with their speed, racking up large numbers of strikeouts in the process. (Pitchers who are not mainly power pitchers can record substantial numbers of strikeouts, too, but they do it more by deception than by raw speed, and their strikeout totals are usually considerably less.)

Walter Johnson led the league in strikeouts twelve times, and Vance, Grove, Feller, and Ryan seven times each. Even mainly power pitchers, however, usually develop a curve and change of pace (or slow ball), so that the contrast makes their fast ball look even faster.

Although Walter Johnson and Lefty Grove went through most of their careers without much of a curve, Dazzy Vance, Bob Feller, Sandy Koufax, and Nolan Ryan all perfected outstanding curves that eventually became as important as their fast ball. The combination of a blazing fast ball *and* a sharp-breaking curve, along with a change of pace, made them practically unhittable when everything was working right.

Does a curve ball *really* curve, or is it an optical illusion? This question used to be debated all the time. Now it is generally agreed that the spin a pitcher puts on a baseball by snapping his wrist when he releases the ball really does make it curve. This conclusion is supported by proof from the principles of physics and aerodynamics.

And, of course, all pitchers, no matter what kind, need *control*—the ability to throw the ball where they want to when they want to. For a pitch to be in the strike zone, it must be over home plate and between the batter's armpits and the top of his knees when he is in his normal batting stance.

Before Eddie Gaedel, the 3 foot 7 inch midget, came to bat in

Tom Seaver

1951, St. Louis owner Bill Veeck taught him to crouch over as much as possible when taking his batting stance. The result was a strike zone that measured exactly 1½ inches!

However, when Eddie actually came up to bat, he ignored Veeck's instructions and stood more or less straight up, with his feet spread wide, imitating Joe DiMaggio's batting stance. He walked on four straight pitches, anyway.

When ballplayers sit around and talk among themselves and the subject of control comes up, sooner or later Steve Dalkowski's name is sure to be mentioned. Although most baseball fans never heard of him, Steve Dalkowski is a legend among ballplayers.

A left-handed pitcher from New Britain, Connecticut, Dalkowski is said to have been the fastest pitcher who ever lived, with no exceptions. Those who saw him swear that his fast ball flashed by at a speed of well *over* 100 miles an hour!

Dalkowski pitched in the minor leagues from 1957 to 1965 but never made it to the big leagues because he could not master control. In nine years in the minors, he pitched about 1,000 innings and struck out 1,400 batters. But he walked as many as he struck out, so that his lifetime ERA was 5.59. He lost almost twice as many games as he won and quit baseball in disgust at the age of twenty-six.

Feller, Koufax, and Nolan Ryan all had control problems, too, at one time or another. Feller led the league in bases on balls four times, Ryan seven times. Ryan also led the league in wild pitches three times.

Even pitchers who do *not* rely primarily on their fast ball, and that includes most of them, need at least an 80–85-mile-an-hour fast ball to pitch successfully in the big leagues.

Steve Dalkowski

Nolan Ryan, the only man ever to pitch five no-hitters

Without it, batters of major league quality would soon learn to time their "breaking" pitches—such as their curve, slider, screwball, knuckleball, sinker, or what have you—and hit them solidly. By mixing up their pitches—sometimes a curve, occasionally a fast ball, unexpectedly a slow ball or change of pace— they throw the batter's timing off, making all of their pitches more difficult to hit.

Gene Conley, who pitched for the Braves, Phillies, and Red Sox in the 1950s and early 1960s, was one of the tallest pitchers in the history of the game. He was 6 feet 8 inches tall and weighed 225 pounds. For a number of years, he played professional basketball with the Boston Celtics when the baseball season ended and then returned to big league baseball when the basketball season finished.

Although he was not mainly a fast-ball pitcher, Conley realized the importance of his fast ball in making all his pitches effective. In 1964, he hurt his arm and could no longer put much speed on his pitches. After months of trying, he finally gave up, and years later he described how he felt at the time.

"I walked into a church," he recalled, "and sat down in the back, all by myself. There was a service going on. All of a sudden, it hit me real hard, and I started crying. I just sat there in that last row and cried and cried, trying to keep my head down so as not to upset anybody. Then I felt a hand on my shoulder, and I looked up. An elderly gentleman was standing there, gazing down at me. 'What's the matter, son?' he asked. 'Did you lose your mother?' I shook my head, the tears still running. 'No, sir,' I said. 'I lost my fast ball.' "

>>>

FIELDING

"What Night Shall We Make It, Al?"

Fielding is the most underrated part of baseball. Great hitters and great pitchers become famous, but great fielders don't even make it to the big leagues unless they can also hit reasonably well.

Mike Gonzalez, a Cuban-born scout for the St. Louis Cardinals in the 1930s, spoke only broken English. Once he sent a famous telegram back to St. Louis after scouting a minor league prospect: "Good field, no hit," read the telegram, and that was the end of that prospect.

Defense is rarely as spectacular as offense no matter what the sport. But good fielding *does* win ball games just as poor fielding loses them.

The defensive brilliance of third baseman Brooks Robinson of the Baltimore Orioles was crucial in winning the 1970 World Series. The same is true of the sparkling defensive play of Yankee third baseman Graig Nettles in the 1978 World Series. On the other hand, a line drive misjudged by St. Louis Cardinals' center fielder Curt Flood was the turning point in the seventh game of the 1968 World Series when the Detroit Tigers beat the Cardinals by a score of 4-1 to win the series.

Let's consider the defensive positions one by one and examine each in turn.

108

The *catcher* is the team's field general. Although the protective equipment he wears is often called "the tools of ignorance," in fact the catcher has to be one of the smartest players on the team. He calls the pitches that the pitcher throws—the usual signals are one finger for a fastball, two for a curve, three for a change of pace, and so on. If the pitcher disagrees or wants to throw a different pitch, he either shakes his head or wiggles his glove a few times.

Since batters usually try to anticipate what kind of pitch is coming, pitchers sometimes shake their head not because they really disagree with the catcher but to confuse the batter. They eventually throw the same pitch the catcher first called for, but by that time the batter has had second thoughts.

Catcher Thurman Munson tensely awaits both the ball and the baserunner, who has rounded third and is racing for home.

To call a game well, a catcher has to know the strengths and weaknesses of all the opposing batters and the strengths and weaknesses of his own pitchers. He evaluates one against the other when deciding what pitch to call for under differing circumstances.

The catcher also has to be able to stop low pitches that hit the ground before they reach him. Since a lot of pitchers are low-ball pitchers—that is, their most effective pitches cross home plate around the batter's knees and are dropping when they cross the plate—the ball sometimes hits the ground before it gets to the catcher. It takes considerable skill to catch or block such pitches so they don't get by and allow base runners to advance.

And, above all, a catcher must have a superb throwing arm in order to prevent base runners from stealing. The distance from home plate to second base is about 127 feet. If a catcher can't make that throw on a line, like a bullet, he'll never be able to stop good base runners from stealing second whenever they feel like it.

Often catchers try to distract the batter by talking to him when he is up at bat. The New York Yankees' Yogi Berra, for example, kept up a steady stream of conversation with one batter after another.

A classic story concerns Boston catcher Al Spohrer, who once tried to distract the great Rogers Hornsby by talking about one of Hornsby's favorite subjects—food.

"Say, Rog," said Spohrer when Hornsby came to bat with two men on base in a close game, "my wife has discovered a butcher who has fantastic steaks."

"Is that so?" responded Hornsby.

"Strike one!" the umpire said.

"Not only that, Rog, but you know how great a cook my wife is," continued Spohrer.

"Strike two!" said the umpire.

"We thought," Spohrer went on, "that maybe you'd like to come over to the house and have dinner with us some night."

Crack! Hornsby walloped the ball over the left-field fence and then trotted around the bases. As he crossed home plate, he turned toward a dejected Spohrer.

"What night shall we make it, Al?" he asked.

The *first baseman* is often a slugger whose fielding might leave something to be desired. Nevertheless, there have been many good-hitting *and* sharp-fielding first basemen in baseball history. A good-fielding first baseman can add a great deal to a team's defense because many left-handed batters hit hard ground balls somewhere in the neighborhood of first base. A first baseman who can snare these and turn them into outs will prevent a lot of runs from scoring.

The main job of the first baseman, however, is to be a vacuum cleaner in gobbling up poor throws. Many of the throws to him are in the dirt or wide or high because they come from infielders who are off balance when they hurriedly release the ball. If a first baseman can't handle wild throws that are reachable, he won't last long in the big leagues. Not at first base, anyway.

The first baseman must also have the flexibility of a ballet dancer because he has to stretch as far as humanly possible when receiving throws from the other infielders who are trying to get the ball to him before the runner arrives at first base. The farther

First baseman Steve Garvey stretches to backhand a throw that has bounced about ten feet in front of him. (The baserunner is Frank Taveras.)

he stretches, the quicker the ball reaches his glove, and in many plays at first base only a fraction of a second is the difference between safe and out.

It is desirable, but not absolutely necessary, that a first baseman throw left-handed. It is easier, and quicker, for a left-handed first baseman to pick up a bunt or a ground ball and throw to second base to start a first-to-second-to-first double play.

If you stop to think about it, you take a forward step with your *left foot* when you throw *right-handed*. And you similarly take a forward step with your *right foot* when you throw *left-handed*.

When a left-handed first baseman picks up a ground ball, his *right* foot is already on his second-base side. So all he has to do is throw the ball to second base. But when a right-handed first baseman picks up a ground ball, his *left* foot is on the wrong side; it is on the first-base side. So he has to turn completely around to throw to second base.

Nevertheless, some of baseball's greatest first basemen were right-handed—like Jimmie Foxx, Hank Greenberg, and Steve Garvey.

The *second baseman* has to be an acrobat with nerves of steel. He has to be able to execute a double play even though he knows a base runner he can't see may crash into him momentarily. He has to be a sure fielder on ground balls, of course, and able to range far to either his right or left. But what distinguishes the best second basemen from the merely good ones is their ability to make the short-to-second-to-first double play.

On the most common double play, the shortstop fields a ground ball and tosses it to the second baseman, who steps on second and relays the ball to first. As the second baseman takes the toss from the shortstop, his back or left side is toward first base so he cannot see how close the base runner from first base is to him. But he knows that something closely resembling a freight train is bearing down on him and may smash into him at any second. Despite this, he has to touch second base, jump over the sliding base runner, and throw to first base all at once.

Unlike the first baseman, the second baseman has no choice: he *must* throw right-handed. Otherwise, he could never make that particular play quickly enough. Since his left foot is already closer to first base than his right foot when he touches second base, a right-handed second baseman doesn't have to turn all the way around before relaying the ball to the first baseman.

A lot of times, the second baseman doesn't actually *touch* second base on that play. But as long as he comes fairly close, the umpire usually lets him get away with it. Umpires have a certain amount of sympathy for the second baseman and give him a break—they know that if the second baseman doesn't get out of the way quickly, he'll be flattened by the oncoming base runner,

Jerry Coleman of the Yankees shows why a second baseman has to be an acrobat with nerves of steel. (The baserunner, out at second as the first part of a double play, is Jerry Scala of the White Sox.)

who is eager to break up the double play. These are called "phantom" double plays, but they count just as much as the "real" ones.

When the *shortstop* is the middle man on a double play, at least he is facing first base and can see the base runner coming toward him. In all other respects, however, the shortstop has the toughest job in the infield. Since about two out of every three hitters bat right-handed, more ground balls are hit into the shortstop's territory than anywhere else.

In fact, the shortstop is so important defensively that he is an exception to the rule that great fielders don't make it to the big leagues unless they can also hit reasonably well. A brilliant defensive shortstop can last for years in the major leagues even if he isn't very productive on offense. (Sometimes that holds for a very good defensive catcher, too.)

The crucial play for a shortstop, the one play that separates a truly great shortstop from all the rest, is fielding a ground ball deep "in the hole," that is, far back and well over to his right. This requires speed, agility, and an exceptionally long and strong throw to first base, a throw of about 130 or 135 feet. He has to backhand the ball while running *away* from first base, set himself, and fire it to the first baseman with enough power so it gets there ahead of the runner.

Like second basemen, shortstops *must* throw right-handed. Otherwise, they could never make that particular play in time. Since their left foot is already closer to first base than their right foot on that play, right-handed shortstops don't have to waste time turning all the way around before throwing the ball to the first baseman.

The introduction of artificial turf has made all the defensive positions more difficult to play than they used to be because ground balls roll much faster on synthetic turf than they do on grass. All the infielders have to play farther back on artificial turf than on grass, or else the ball is past them before they have time to react. On the other hand, they worry less about bad hops on artificial turf.

Cincinnati shortstop Dave Concepcion devised an ingenious way of using artificial turf to his own advantage. On long throws from deep in the hole, he perfected the tactic of deliberately throwing the ball into the turf about 15 feet in front of the first baseman, letting one long bounce carry it the rest of the way. This isn't possible on grass except as a last resort because the bounce isn't as true and the ball rarely accelerates when it hits real grass the way it often does when it hits artificial turf.

Although speed is an asset to a shortstop, knowledge about where to play the batters can compensate to a great extent when a shortstop isn't too fast afoot. Indeed, all good fielders, no matter what position they play, depend as much on their knowledge of *where* to play each batter as on anything else. They will shift several feet to the right or left or backwards or forwards, depending on the batter's typical hitting pattern, the pitcher's characteristics, the type of pitch coming up, and any other factors that could influence where the ball might be hit.

The *third baseman* has to have an instantaneous reaction time because many of the balls hit to him are line drives or very hard grounders that reach him in a flash. He either grabs the ball almost instinctively, or he doesn't.

Baltimore third baseman Brooks Robinson makes a routine play.

Pepper Martin, who played third base for the St. Louis Cardinals in the 1930s, used his chest as much as his glove in fielding his position. He'd block the ball with his body, pounce on it, and throw to first base.

The third baseman's most difficult play is a bunt or slow roller down the third-base line. He has to dash in, grab the ball with his bare hand, and whip it over to first base, all in one fluid motion. Again, third basemen have to throw right-handed. Otherwise, they would have no chance of executing that play in time to get the runner. Since a third baseman's left foot is closer to first base than his right foot, a right-handed third baseman doesn't have to turn all the way around to throw the ball to first base.

There have been only a few great fielding third basemen in

history because the position is often filled—like first base—with a good hitter whose fielding is only passable. Pie Traynor, of the Pittsburgh Pirates in the 1920s and early 1930s, was one of the best. At the time the saying was "Twice Hornsby doubled down the left-field line and twice Traynor threw him out."

Other outstanding fielding third basemen include Billy Cox of the Brooklyn Dodgers, Brooks Robinson of the Baltimore Orioles, Clete Boyer and Graig Nettles of the New York Yankees, and Mike Schmidt of the Philadelphia Phillies.

The *outfielders* are generally the big hitters. A good-fielding outfielder can be enormously helpful to a team, but good hitters who can't field have to be fitted in *somewhere*. Unless they're designated hitters, who never play defensively, they usually wind up in the outfield—especially if they throw left-handed and can't play first base. (Actually, *anyone* who throws left-handed and can't pitch or play first base will necessarily wind up in the outfield.)

The best outfielder—usually the fastest—will generally be the *center fielder*. He has the most territory to cover, and if the right and left fielders are not fully reliable, the center fielder will have to patrol a good deal of right-center and left-center as well as center field itself. He has to be fast, able to come in for balls hit over the second baseman's and shortstop's heads, able to go back for long fly balls, and have a good enough arm to make long and accurate throws to third base and home plate when needed.

Many believe that Willie Mays was the greatest defensive center fielder of all time. His most famous catch was in the 1954 World Series when Cleveland's Vic Wertz hit a towering fly ball 460 feet to deep center field. Running at top speed with his back

Willie Mays snares Vic Wertz's 460-foot drive to deep center field in the
1954 World Series.

to home plate, Mays caught it over his left shoulder and in one fluid motion whirled around and threw the ball back to the infield. Instead of two men scoring, none did, and the Giants went on to win the game and the Series.

Actually, the *right fielder* needs to have an even *better* arm than the center fielder, since he frequently has to make the very long throw from right field to third base to keep base runners from going from first to third on a single. Babe Ruth, Roberto Clemente, Carl Furillo, and Al Kaline all played right field most of the time because of their exceptional throwing abilities.

By the way, it isn't just the distance that is important on a long throw from the outfield. Equally important is the trajectory—that is, the throw shouldn't be a high one that arcs like a rainbow from the outfielder to its destination. It should be a *low* throw, on a line about 7 or 8 feet high almost its entire length so that an infielder (the cutoff man) can interrupt it and redirect it somewhere else if necessary. Long, high throws that miss the cutoff man often impress the crowd, but the manager will be less enthusiastic.

The *left fielder* will often be the team's weakest fielder both in terms of speed and throwing proficiency. This doesn't mean that all left fielders are poor defensive outfielders. Far from it. But if a team does happen to have a hard-hitting outfielder who isn't too fast and can't throw too well, he'll be its designated hitter or left fielder.

Artificial turf puts even more pressure on outfielders than on infielders. Since the ball moves so much faster on artificial turf than on grass, outfielders have to be faster than ever to stop it from getting past them. What would ordinarily be a single on real grass can easily become a between-the-outfielders triple on synthetic turf if the outfielders aren't quick enough to get to the ball before it skips by them and rolls all the way to the fence.

One of the most unusual outfielders of all time was Pete Gray, who played 77 games for St. Louis in the American League in 1945, during World War II. What made Pete so unusual was that he had only one arm.

Pete Gray was born in Nanticoke, Pennsylvania, in 1917. At the age of six, he lost his right arm in an accident. It was amputated just below the shoulder. Nevertheless, he was determined to be a ballplayer, and by perseverance and practice he taught himself to catch, throw, and bat with only his left arm.

Pete Gray at
Yankee Stadium
in 1945

He played in the minor leagues in 1942, 1943, and 1944, batting .333 with Memphis in the Southern Association in 1944 and handling over 340 chances in the outfield with only 6 errors. That earned him a chance in the big leagues.

How did Pete Gray manage to function in the outfield with only one arm?

He would catch the ball with his left (gloved) hand, place the ball against his chest, let it roll out of his glove and up his wrist as he tucked the glove under the stub of his right arm, and then draw his left arm back across his chest until the ball rolled back into his hand. He became so adept at this maneuver that he could return the ball to the infield almost as quickly as an ordinary outfielder.

But big league pitching proved too much for him, and he batted only .218 in 77 games in 1945. He went back to the minors where he played until he retired in 1949, at the age of thirty-two. His lifetime minor league batting average was a very respectable .308.

Like infielders, outfielders have to play each batter differently, moving in or out or to one side or the other, depending on who is at bat, who is pitching, what the next pitch is going to be, how the wind is blowing, and so on. Even though it might look like they are just hanging around out there until a ball is hit in their direction, they are alert and thinking on every pitch. (Well, most of them are, anyway.)

Occasionally, however, an outfielder may let his mind wander a bit, especially if he is tired. In 1934, Hack Wilson, the stocky home-run hitter (5 feet 6 and 195 pounds), was playing right field for the Brooklyn Dodgers. It was a hot, muggy day, and Boom-Boom Beck was pitching for Brooklyn. He wasn't called Boom-Boom for nothing, and on this particular afternoon he was getting hit pretty hard. Line drives were rattling off the tin advertising signs on the right-field wall above Hack's head one after the other, and he was getting exhausted chasing the ball and throwing it back to the infield.

Hack Wilson with the Brooklyn Dodgers in 1934

Finally, Casey Stengel, who was managing the Dodgers that year, came out to the mound to change pitchers. Taking advantage of the pause in the game, Hack tried to rest as well as he could out in right field—his hands on his knees, staring down at the grass, trying to catch his breath.

But the unhappy Boom-Boom, instead of handing the ball to Stengel, angrily threw it with all his might out to right field, taking his frustrations out on the baseball.

Hearing the familiar sound of a ball hitting a tin sign above his head, the startled Hack awoke from his daydreams and assumed the game had begun again. As the crowd watched in amusement, he ran after the ball as fast as he could, retrieved it, and fired it on a line to second base, a perfect throw to get the runner—if only there had been one!

STRATEGY

How to Be a Big League Manager
in One Easy Lesson

Baseball games are fun to watch because you're rooting for your team to win. A home run by your team is great, and one by the other team is terrible. But, in addition, a lot of other things are happening that are also fun to know about. Once you become familiar with them, you'll enjoy the game even more (provided, of course, that your team wins).

Take the batting order, for instance. Once the manager hands it to the home-plate umpire, right before the game starts, it's fixed for that game and can't be changed. Substitutions can be made, but the substitutes have to replace specifically someone in the original batting order and bat in that person's place. And once a player has been taken out of a game, he cannot play again in that particular game.

The manager doesn't make out his batting order by pulling numbers out of a hat. He has nine players—ten if there is a designated hitter who bats in place of the pitcher—and he wants to have them coming to bat in a sequence that he figures will produce the most runs.

The leadoff man, the first man up in the batting order, is usually the team's fastest runner. His job is to get on base any way he can as often as possible. He's likely to be a singles-type hitter who coaxes a lot of bases on balls, bunts frequently, and once he gets on first base will be a threat to steal second. Rickey Henderson, Lou Brock and Maury Wills all batted leadoff, for example.

Second place in the batting order is usually reserved for the team's best place hitter. Typically, he's a good hitter who doesn't strike out often. The first and second men in the batting order will tend to score a lot of runs (hopefully), but they won't rank very high in runs batted in because they have less opportunity to drive in runs than those who follow them.

Third, fourth, and fifth are the power hitters, the big men who are capable of hitting the ball over the fence. They are relied on to drive in the runs. The number-three batter is often the team's best hitter in terms of batting average *and* power, while the fourth and fifth are more strictly power oriented. Babe Ruth and Roberto Clemente usually batted third in the batting order.

It is impossible to generalize on this, however, because Joe Di-Maggio almost always batted fourth, in what has traditionally been called the "cleanup" spot. Many power hitters consider it an honor to be the cleanup batter, with special responsibility for clearing the bases and driving in runs. Historically, though, just as many great hitters have batted third in the batting order as fourth.

The sixth through ninth places are always filled by the weaker hitters. This is so if only because the higher a player is in the batting order, the more times he will come to bat in a game. During the course of an entire season, the top half of the batting order will come to bat over a hundred times more than the bottom half.

Yankee manager Casey Stengel

A manager wants his best hitters to have the most chances to hit.

Other factors also have to be taken into account. For example, if the opposing pitcher is a lefty, then it is better to have right-handed batters facing him. Remember: left-handed batters hit righties best, while right-handed batters hit lefties best. Many managers alternate (or platoon) two players at one or more positions, starting the right-handed batter when the opposing pitcher is a lefty and starting the left-handed batter when the opposing pitcher is a righty.

Once a batter makes it to first base, of course, the idea is to get him all the way around the bases to score a run. It's runs that are important, not hits. If a team has a lot of good power hitters, the manager is likely to play it safe and just wait for a big hit to drive a base runner in.

But if a team is short on good power hitters, or if they strike out too much, other strategies may be necessary. A favorite is the famous *hit-and-run play,* which is intended to move a runner from first base all the way to third on a single.

With the hit-and-run play, the man on first base takes off for second as soon as the pitcher starts to throw the ball toward home plate. Thinking the base runner is trying to steal second, the second baseman (or the shortstop) dashes over to second base to take the throw from the catcher. The batter's job is to then hit the ball through the part of the infield just vacated by the second baseman (or the shortstop). It really should be called the run-and-hit play rather than the hit-and-run, because the base runner starts running before the batter hits the ball.

The batter's chances of hitting safely are increased because the second baseman (or the shortstop) has left his normal defensive position unguarded. And if the batter does get a hit, the man on first base should easily make it all the way around to third on a single because he has had such a big head start.

The hit-and-run is also helpful in keeping the batter from hitting into a double play on a ground ball. Nothing takes the steam out of a rally faster than someone hitting into a double play. Since the man on first is already well on his way to second base by the time the ball is hit, he's likely to get there safely even if the batter hits a hard ground ball directly at an infielder, a grounder that, with a man on first, would normally result in a double play.

If the hit-and-run is such a great play, then why isn't it used all the time? Because there are risks involved in using it. Unless the batter is a really good place hitter who can hit the ball *on the ground,* it's a dangerous play.

If the batter hits a line drive at an infielder or a not very high infield fly ball, the hit-and-run turns into a sure double play. After catching it, the infielder can easily throw to first base for a double play before the runner can get back. And if the batter misses the ball entirely or fails to swing at it, perhaps because he missed a sign, the catcher can throw the base runner out at second base.

Indeed, if the catcher anticipates that a hit-and-run play is coming up, he'll signal the pitcher to throw a *pitchout*—a pitch that comes in shoulder high and a few feet wide of home plate, where the batter can't reach it—and then the catcher can throw the surprised runner out at second.

It is obvious that signs from the manager to the players are very important on the hit-and-run play and on all other special plays as well. Both the batter and the base runner have to know that the play is "on" for the next pitch. A story is often told about a major league batter who failed to swing at a pitch under such circumstances, so that the man on first was easily thrown out at second.

When the batter came back to the bench, the manager asked him very patiently, "Do you know that when I scratch my nose, that's the hit-and-run sign?"

"Yes," said the player.

"Did you see me scratching my nose?" the manager asked.

"Yes," said the player.

"Then why the heck didn't you try to hit the ball?"

"I didn't think you really meant it," the player answered.

The coaches at first and third base often relay the signs from the manager to the players. That is usually the job of the third-base coach, which is why you will frequently see a batter take a long hard look toward third base before getting set in the batter's box.

Another popular strategy to advance a runner from first base is the *sacrifice bunt*. With a man on first base and fewer than two men out, the manager tells the batter to sacrifice the base runner to second. It's called a sacrifice because what the batter does is "sacrifice" himself, or give up his own chance to get a hit, in order to move the runner from first to second base for the good of the team.

The batter does this by bunting the ball *on the ground* so it rolls 25 or 30 feet into the infield. He is usually thrown out at first, but by that time the runner has moved to second where he is now in scoring position—that is, where he has a good chance of scoring even on a single, if it's a long one.

Not all bunts are sacrifices. Often a batter who is fast will bunt to try to get on first base. The difference between bunting for a hit and a sacrifice bunt is that the main idea of a sacrifice bunt is to move the base runner on first base to second base. It is *expected* that the batter will be thrown out at first.

Sometimes when a batter lays down a good sacrifice bunt and gets thrown out at first base, the fans give him a big hand as he trots back to the dugout. Others wonder why all the applause—after all, he's out, isn't he? The reason for the applause is that he's done his job and done it well: he's advanced the runner to second base, which is exactly what he was supposed to do.

There are two problems with a sacrifice bunt. The first is that it automatically gives up an out unless an infielder makes an error. Outs are precious because it takes only three of them to retire the side.

The second problem is that very few ballplayers are good bunters nowadays. They either bunt the ball too hard and too far, resulting in a double play, or they pop it up in the air and it is caught as a fly ball, with the runner unable to advance. More close games are lost in the late innings because of failures to sacrifice successfully than for any other reason.

One special bunting situation, and one of the most exciting plays in baseball, is called the *squeeze play.* With a man on *third* base and less than two out, the batter bunts the ball on the ground, and the base runner takes off and tries to score on the bunt. The squeeze play has two forms: the suicide squeeze and the safety squeeze.

With the *suicide squeeze,* the man on third starts running for home as soon as the pitcher throws the ball. If the batter makes any kind of decent bunt at all—that is, if he doesn't pop the ball up in the air or miss it completely—the base runner is almost certain to slide across home plate safely. On the other hand, if the batter fails to bunt the ball—if he pops it up or misses it, perhaps because the catcher called for a pitchout—then the base runner is a sure out.

If a right-handed batter misses the sign on *this* play, by the way, somebody could get hurt. If he misses the sign and just lets the pitch go by, he's going to be awfully surprised to hear the pounding feet of his own teammate racing for home right behind him. Or if he swings hard and hits a line drive down the third-base line, he could practically tear the head off the base runner, who'll be halfway to home by then.

If a left-handed batter misses the sign on a suicide squeeze play, he's at least facing third base and will see that *something* is going on and be able to get out of the way.

With the *safety squeeze,* the man on third base is more cautious. He waits until he sees the batter actually bunt the ball on the ground, and *then* he takes off for home. It's less risky than the suicide squeeze, but the bunt has to be better (or the base runner faster) because the base runner has gotten a later start. Both squeeze plays are exciting, but neither one is seen very often because so few batters can be counted on to bunt well.

The hit-and-run, sacrifice bunt, and squeeze play are all *offensive* plays. Their purpose is to help score runs. But managers also spend a lot of time thinking about *defensive* strategy—how to stop the other team from scoring.

The pitchout, for example, is a defensive maneuver. When the manager of the team in the field anticipates a hit-and-run play by the team up at bat or an attempt to steal a base, he can signal for a pitchout. This enables the catcher to throw the base runner out and spoil a potential rally.

One defensive tactic that always gets boos from fans of the team up at bat is an *intentional walk.* The pitcher throws four balls in a row, each well wide of the plate, and the batter trots to first base. Why would a manager ever tell his pitcher to walk an opposing batter on purpose?

One possible reason is that the batter is so dangerous the manager would rather pitch to the next man in the batting order. It's no accident that the all-time leaders in bases on balls are Babe Ruth and Ted Williams.

Just as often, however, it is done because base runners are already on second and third and first base is open. The manager *wants* to load the bases because that sets up the possibility of a defensive play—*a force-out at any base*—that is not possible unless first base is occupied. With the bases full, all base runners are forced to run when the batter hits a ground ball because two men can't be on one base at the same time—they have to run to make room for the advancing base runners behind them.

This means that a base runner can now be forced out by an infielder fielding a ground ball and just stepping on any base, including home plate, before the runner gets there. If this sounds complicated, remember that it happens all the time with the familiar second-base-to-first-base double play, where the shortstop or second baseman only has to touch second to force out the runner coming down from first. The runner is forced out because the batter who hit the ground ball is advancing to take over first base.

When first base is unoccupied, on the other hand, no force-out is possible. If the batter hits a ground ball, the base runners on second and third can simply stay put if they want to.

It is also easier to make a double play when the bases are filled than when runners are only on second and third. With the bases

Philadelphia manager Connie Mack is offered a flower by a young admirer in exchange for an autographed baseball. Slugger Jimmie Foxx is obviously intrigued.

loaded, an infielder with the ball can step on *any* base to force a runner and then throw to first base to get the batter. Again, if first base had been unoccupied, no force-out would have been possible anywhere.

For these reasons, if base runners are already on second and third, it often makes sense to deliberately walk the batter and put someone on first base, too. This is especially true if the batter is a dangerous hitter and it is late in the game. You can still boo if the opposing manager does it to your favorite home-run slugger, but now you'll understand why he's doing it.

Of course, like all strategies, both offensive and defensive, it doesn't always work. If the next batter hits a home run with the bases loaded, the manager doesn't look too smart. Babe Ruth was followed in the New York Yankee batting order by Lou Gehrig, and many times the Babe was intentionally walked when men were already on second and third. It probably worked some of the time but not all of the time: Lou Gehrig hit an all-time record 23 home runs with the bases loaded!

Everything considered, how important is a manager to the success of a baseball team?

There have been many famous managers in baseball history— Connie Mack, John McGraw, Frank Chance, and Casey Stengel, to name but four. All of them had losing as well as winning years.

Connie Mack managed the Philadelphia Athletics for fifty years, from 1901 through 1950. When he retired, in 1950, he was eighty-seven years old. A catcher in his playing days, Connie won nine pennants and five World Series, but he also finished last in the American League *seventeen* times. How could he remain as

Manager John McGraw of the Giants, left, and Babe Ruth of the Yankees shake hands before the start of the 1921 World Series. The two never cared much for each other.

manager so long if he finished last so many times? It's simple: he owned the team.

John J. McGraw managed the New York Giants from 1902 to 1932. He won ten pennants and three World Series, and finished last in the National League twice. A scrappy manager who previously had been an outstanding third baseman, he believed in bunting, place hitting, and stealing bases. He could never adapt to the lively ball and the home-run hitting it stimulated. When Babe Ruth was still a pitcher but playing in the outfield occasionally as well, McGraw's only comment about Ruth was "If he plays every day, the bum will hit into a hundred double plays a season."

Frank Chance was player-manager of the pennant-winning Chicago Cubs in 1906, 1907, 1908, and 1910. He was the first baseman of the famous Tinker to Evers to Chance double-play combination of those years. As manager of the Cubs and later of the Yankees and Red Sox, he won four pennants and two World Series and also finished last once.

Casey Stengel knew both the highs and the lows. He won ten pennants and seven World Series as manager of the New York Yankees, including a record five World Series in a row from 1949 through 1953. But as manager of the New York Mets from 1962 to 1965, he finished last every year.

Everything considered, how important is a manager to the success of a baseball team?

Listen to Lefty O'Doul, a great hitter in the 1920s and early 1930s, who had a .349 lifetime batting average. "I played for a lot of managers in my day," he once said, "including John McGraw, Frank Chance, and Miss Rosie Stultz. The most successful of all was Rosie Stultz. She was our seventh-grade teacher at Bay View

Manager and former first baseman Frank Chance

Grammar School, and she managed the school team. We won the grade-school championship of San Francisco in 1912 with Miss Rosie Stultz managing.

"A manager can only do so much," O'Doul continued. "The rest is up to the players. It's the players who make the manager, not the other way around. I managed for twenty-four years myself in the minor leagues, in the Pacific Coast League. In 1935, I had Joe DiMaggio playing in the outfield and won the pennant. He hit .398. He was sold to the Yankees that winter, and the next year I finished next to last. Do you want another example? Take Frank Chance. He was one of the greatest, right? He won all those pennants with the Chicago Cubs. Well, Frank Chance was my manager on the Boston Red Sox in 1923, and where do you think we finished? Dead last, that's where.

"Which just goes to prove," O'Doul concluded, "if you haven't got the players, you haven't got a chance!"

>>

WHY IS BASEBALL SO POPULAR?

Why has baseball remained so popular for all these years? Since Alexander Cartwright first laid out the dimensions of the playing field and drew up the rules of the game, it has furnished enjoyment and excitement for countless millions of people, young and old alike.

Some believe the continued popularity of baseball is because it is a uniquely American game. But baseball is an important part of daily life not only in America but also in countries as diverse as Japan, Mexico, Venezuela, the Dominican Republic, and Cuba. Not to mention Puerto Rico, which is part of the United States but has its own cultural heritage.

If you think about it from a broader perspective, it isn't really Hank Aaron, with 755 lifetime home runs, who is the all-time home-run king. It's left-handed hitting Sadaharu Oh, first baseman of Tokyo's Yomiuri Giants, who hit his 756th home run on September 3, 1977. He retired in 1980, with 868 lifetime home runs. The son of a Chinese father and a Japanese mother, Oh is one of Japan's national heroes.

The 1981 pitching sensation of the Los Angeles Dodgers was Fernando Valenzuela from Sonora, Mexico. Cincinnati shortstop

Japan's Sadaharu Oh, the leading home run hitter of all time

Dave Concepcion was born and raised in Aragua, Venezuela. Pitching star Juan Marichal of the San Francisco Giants was born in the Dominican Republic. Roberto Clemente was from Puerto Rico. Pitcher Luis Tiant came from Cuba.

So it is not anything uniquely American about the game that accounts for its widespread and continued popularity.

Perhaps it is because baseball is a game that more or less "ordinary" people can play. Professional basketball players have to be very tall and football players very big. Most major league baseball players, however, are about 6 feet tall and weigh around 190 pounds, and many are much smaller.

For example, what do all of the following have in common: Yogi Berra, Roy Campanella, Roberto Clemente, Jimmie Foxx, Rogers Hornsby, Willie Mays, Mel Ott, and Honus Wagner? The answer is that all of them are less than 6 feet tall. And the list includes three men—Jimmie Foxx, Willie Mays, and Mel Ott—who each hit over 500 career home runs.

Or perhaps it is freedom from the restraints of time that accounts for baseball's appeal. Time governs virtually everything we do in life, but it doesn't control baseball games. Baseball is the only team sport that dispenses completely with a clock. A ballgame continues at its own pace for nine innings—more if necessary to determine a winner—regardless of how long it takes.

The fastest big league game ever played took only 51 minutes. The New York Giants beat the Philadelphia Phillies, 6-1, in that length of time on September 28, 1919.

By contrast, the longest major league game ever played took 7 hours and 23 minutes, when the San Francisco Giants beat the New York Mets, 8-6, in a game that went 23 innings on May 31, 1964. It was the second game of a double-header. The first game started at one o'clock in the afternoon, and the second game didn't end until almost 11:30 that night.

The longest game in major league history in terms of *innings* was a 26-inning 1-1 tie between Brooklyn and Boston on May 1, 1920. The starting pitchers, Brooklyn's Leon Cadore and Boston's Joe Oeschger, both pitched the entire distance, the equivalent of almost three full games. The game took 3 hours and 50 minutes and was finally called on account of darkness at ten minutes to seven in the evening. If they had lights back then, there's no telling how long they might have played.

More likely than any of the above, however, in explaining the popularity of the game is the fluctuating drama in baseball that arises out of the succession of confrontations between two lonely people—the pitcher versus the batter. It is a contest of wits, intelligence, skill, and strength. It also involves more than a little courage because the ball is as hard as a rock and often comes toward home plate like a flash of lightning.

The emotional tension ebbs and flows, with fairly long periods of apparent calm suddenly interrupted by bursts of action in which the game rides on every pitch.

A single, a stolen base, an error on an easy play, and all at once what had been a comfortable 4-1 lead no longer looks so safe. The pitcher starts to sweat, the batter feels the weight of responsibility on his shoulders, and the fielders move nervously back and forth smoothing the ground around their positions.

The crowd stops looking for a hot dog vendor and leans forward, rooting noisily or silently for one side or the other, anxiously awaiting the next pitch.

The suspense is heightened by the fact that most of the fans know each of the players as individuals. They have never met the players personally, but they know them better than they know their next-door neighbors—their backgrounds, their salaries, their family problems, their physical and emotional ailments, whether they are easygoing or aggressive, their past successes and failures, and whether their careers are mostly behind or ahead of them.

Teams win or lose, but it is *individuals* who clearly and unmistakeably bear the responsibility for victories or defeats. Baseball is a team game, but it is played by individuals who do their job singly and alone, in the full glare of the spotlight. They will be praised or blamed, become heroes or goats, depending on their performance under pressure.

That's how it was when Christy Mathewson faced Honus Wagner, when Sandy Koufax watched Hank Aaron walking up to the plate, when Nolan Ryan looked down from the pitcher's mound and saw the menacing figure of Willie Stargell.

The contest between pitcher and batter is the same now as it was a hundred years ago. Human strengths and weaknesses are tested, and not only the teams but also the fans win or lose depending on the outcome. Its appeal is evidently both universal and timeless.

Bob Feller pitching to Joe DiMaggio (on April 30, 1946)

Many of the photographs in this book are from The Card Memorabilia Associates in Peekskill, New York, and from the National Baseball Hall of Fame and Museum in Cooperstown, New York. I am deeply indebted to Michael P. Aronstein, President of TCMA, and to Jack Redding, Librarian of the Baseball Hall of Fame, for their kind assistance.

I am equally grateful to Nat Andriani, of United Press International, and to Don Bowden, of Wide World Photos, both of whom generously went out of their way to be both pleasant and helpful.

Aside from the photographs from TCMA and the Hall of Fame, the others are from the following sources:

BALTIMORE ORIOLES: 105
ROBERT C. BARTOSZ, Pennsauken, New Jersey: 60
BROWN BROTHERS, Sterling, Pennsylvania: 10, 138
CULVER PICTURES, New York: 9, 22, 99
NANCY HOGUE, Warren, Ohio: 69 (bottom), 75 (top), 86, 103
    (top), 112
RICHARD KAVESH, Upper Montclair, New Jersey: 141
RONALD C. MODRA, Port Washington, Wisconsin: 69 (top)
NEW YORK DAILY NEWS: 119
NEW YORK HISTORICAL SOCIETY: 2
PHILADELPHIA PHILLIES (Paul H. Roedig, Photogapher):
    91 (bottom)
LOUIS REQUENA, Little Ferry, New Jersey: 100 (bottom), 103
    (bottom), 117
UNITED PRESS INTERNATIONAL: 36, 58, 64, 66, 75 (bottom), 88
    (top), 88 (bottom), 98, 121, 145
WIDE WORLD PHOTOS: 44, 63

Lawrence S. Ritter is the author of *The Glory of Their Times: The Story of the Early Days of Baseball Told by the Men Who Played It,* called "the best sports book in recent memory" by the *New York Times Book Review* and "one of the best baseball books ever published" by *The Sporting News.* He is also the coauthor (with Donald Honig) of *The Image of Their Greatness* and *The 100 Greatest Baseball Players of All Time.* In addition, Mr. Ritter is a professor of economics and finance and former chairman of the department of finance at the Graduate School of Business Administration of New York University.